We shall be all

The contributors to this collection of essays on recent
Scottish working class history are: Vincent and Ann
Flynn, both lifelong socialists and trade unionists,
raised in Glasgow after the First World War; John
Leopold, an historian who works with the Workers
Educational Association in Paisley; Dave Sherry, a
Socialist Workers' Party organiser in the west of
Scotland; and Laurie Flynn, who writes for Socialist
Worker.

We shall be all

recent chapters in the history of
working class struggle in Scotland

Bookmarks Glasgow and London

First published 1978 by
Bookmarks
64 Queen Street, Glasgow, and
265 Seven Sisters Road
London N4 2DE
Distributed by
Boom Town Books
King Street, Aberdeen
Copyright © Bookmarks 1978
ISBN 0 906224 00 4

Printed by
A Wheaton and Company,
Typesetting by Printacolor,
Designed by John Finn
Cover photograph
and original photographs by
John Sturrock (Report)

Arise you prisoners of starvation
Arise you wretched of the earth
For justice thunders condemnation
A better world's in birth

No more tradition's chains shall bind us
Arise you slaves no more in thrall
The earth shall rise on new foundations
We have been naught — we shall be all.

From the American version of the great revolutionary
working-class song 'The Internationale'

Contents

Introduction

It is no surprise that attacks on London government are the centre-piece of Scottish Nationalist propaganda. Ordinary people, north *and* south of the border, feel thwarted, cheated and betrayed by the sham democracy of Westminster. They feel thwarted, cheated and betrayed because they have been thwarted, cheated and betrayed.

The nationalist solution to this is simple. It's called Edinburgh government. In place of sleek lawyers, professional politicians, rich businessmen and their placemen running our lives from London, what do the SNP propose? Simple. Sleek lawyers, professional politicians, rich businessmen and their placemen will run our lives from Edinburgh!

There is to be no change in the system of government. And there is to be no significant change in the corrupt and rotten society of which this system of government is a constituent part. Instead, according to the SNP, as soon as we are blessed with a sovereign assembly in Edinburgh, the door will open to a great and glorious future. Alternatively, in the slightly modified version propounded by Jim Sillars and the Scottish Labour Party, a sovereign assembly will at the very least give us the key to that door.

This propaganda is about equivalent to the following: 'Coca Cola is bloody awful for your teeth when it's bottled in London. But once the bottling plant is located at the foot of Edinburgh's Calton Hill, Coca Cola is positively health giving.'

In reality, the failure of 'London government' has little to do with its location. It flows from the fact that the parliamentary system is a surrogate democracy, a substitute for the real thing, designed to fool people rather than give them control over their own lives.

The parliamentary system involves a tiny minority of people. It does nothing, and can do nothing, to give full and everyday expression to the desires of ordinary people to control their destinies. Indeed it serves to mask the real power relations in our society and the day-to-day dictatorships exercised over us by multinational corporations, factory bosses and foremen of every kind, landlords and policemen and, behind them all, the blind economic forces of a society geared to production for profit, not human need.

To a great extent, the failure of 'London government' for working class people is synonymous with the failure and decay of the Labour Party.

That decay is now far advanced. But it is not something that set in only with age. The earliest Labour governments betrayed many of the same symptoms of accommodation and capitulation to the system that we are witnessing in such a dramatic fashion now.

But Labour didn't fail because its focus was Westminster. It failed because its focus was the changing of the system in and through orthodox political institutions — by the many doing little more than electing the few to high position and hoping for the best. Instead of capturing power, Labour captured office. Willingly or unwillingly, Labour's leaders became prisoners of the system.

The fate of the Labour Party is eloquent testimony for the view propounded by two great witnesses of a historic exercise in popular power, the Paris Commune.

'One thing especially was proved by the Commune....,' wrote Karl Marx and Frederick Engels, "that the working class cannot simply lay hold of the ready-made state machinery and wield it for their own purposes...."

Many working-class people in Scotland agree with most, if not all, of the above criticisms of the Labour Party and, by extension, of the SNP and SLP who, with slight modifications, are intent on following Labour down the parliamentary road to nowhere.

Nevertheless, they are still attracted to Edinburgh government. Partly it's because it's a soft option not requiring people to do too much. Partly it's because people do feel that if our masters, or some of them, were nearer in space and time, it would be easier to prod and pressurise them.

But there is another reason for this lingering hope for a parliamentary road to social change. People feel that the alternative is uncharted. Occasionally the socialist alternative does receive some attention. But it is usually portrayed as 'foreign' to the traditions of Scots, Welsh and English workers. In fact, nothing could be further from the truth. The richest episodes, the best traditions in working-class history in these islands, as the essays in this book try to show, point away from passive hope for change from above towards self-activity, self-organisation and socialism from below.

The essays include a study of the great rent struggles of 1915. This shows for the first time just how broad the movement was, and how it was organised by ordinary Glasgow women. Then there is a thorough account of the great struggle for the shorter working week which has enormous relevance for our own time. In the opening contribution, the organisation thrown up in Fife in the course of the General Strike is described in some detail, an organisation all the more significant since it shows in outline how workers can exercise control over their own lives. Then, finally, there is a piece on aspects of the recent history of the working-class movement and how that movement can be developed.

Workers cannot rule society through parliaments and police chiefs. They can only do so with institutions of their own making, institutions which, like Methil's Council of Action in 1926, unlock the energies of the mass of the people. Without them, they cannot even defend their power from the desperate challenge to serious social change that always has come and always will come from big business.

Such a challenge comes because our society is riven with a fundamental and irreconcilable conflict of interest. The SNP are at great pains to deny this. For them, what matters is that we're all Scots.

Yet who can seriously believe that a whisky drinker and a whisky baron have the same interests? And who can believe that the people of Govan, Ferguslie Park or Pilton, or anywhere in between, have any interest in common with Sir Hugh Fraser and the other czars of big business, with the landowning cliques, their associates and friends? Who can believe it when it's plain for all to see that these characters only obtained their wealth and splendour by the subjection and exploitation of the many?

Anyone seeking confirmation of this fact need do no more than trace the whisky back into the boardroom of the Edinburgh-based Distillers Corporation, in one of whose basements, incidentally, the SNP have their head office.

Who will you meet there? Will they be men consumed with schemes for the betterment of civilisation? Or will they be calculating machines driven by the same logistics that drive countless other front men for similar giant capitalist organisations? In the case of Distillers, it isn't too hard to find out. Distillers have never tried to disguise their loyalties in a welter of "Public Relations".

Having marketed an unsafe drug called Thalidomide and caused babies to be born with terrible deformations, these respectable Christian gentlemen knew no remorse. Their 'duty' to 'track records', 'profit projections' and 'rates of return' impelled them to spend ten years trying to cheat those children and their anxious and troubled parents out of the means of living with a measure of financial security to offset the pain. What they did to minimise compensation by way of delay was perfectly legal according to English *and* Scots law, the best in the world. They nearly got away with a £5 million settlement, too. But an explosion of popular protest forced £20 million out of them.

The hard-faced swines of Distillers are not at all untypical of the Scottish section of the ruling class. They are all of them ruthless, arrogant people, used to wealth and power and determined to hang on to what they've got. Some details concerning the extent of their wealth may help explain that determination.

Seven per cent of the population of the United Kingdom own an incredible 84 per cent of its wealth. In Scotland, the inequality is even more grotesque.

'Contrary to the usual myths', writes Michael Fry, economics correspondent of *The Scotsman*, 65 years of so-called redistributive taxation 'have left Scotland a markedly more inegalitarian society than England'. Fry then reveals the following devastating facts on Scotland's two nations:

'Lord Diamond's Royal Commission (on the Distribution of Wealth) found that two-thirds of the Scottish population owned no wealth at all in 1973, or at least none that the Inland Revenue thought worth recording. But only (?) one half of Englishmen had no wealth.

'Even within the category of wealth owners the distribution in Scotland is more unequal. Lord Diamond reported that the richest one per cent owned 28 per cent of all wealth in England but 32 per cent in Scotland. The richest five per cent owned half the wealth in England and nearly two-thirds of it in Scotland. The bottom 80 per cent of wealth holders account for 15 per cent in England, but only five per cent in Scotland.' (No fair shares in the Wealth of a Nation, *The Scotsman*, 5 October 1976)

Fry also quotes from a study by Alan Harrison of Strathclyde University which shows that the stupendous concentration of wealth in Scotland can be illustrated even more dramatically by taking the wealthiest group of all, the top 0.1 per cent of the population.

In 1969, these 3000 people between them owned more than 10 per cent of all wealth, totalling £640 million. And there is every reason to believe that today they own even more, for, as Harrison's study shows, in Scotland since the 1960s there has been a redistribution of wealth from poor to rich. While these people have an average individual fortune of £210,000, pensioners in Glasgow die every winter of the cold because they haven't the wherewithal to pay for enough food and heating to keep them warm.

But even this savage outline of Scotland's two nations underestimates the true extent of the stranglehold these parasites have upon our lives. Just a brief glance at the physical ownership of land in this country makes the inequality even more grotesque.

John McEwen, the retired forestry consultant who has spent years tracking down information on land ownership in the Highlands, has shown that a mere 340 individuals or companies own two-thirds of all the Highlands and Islands of Scotland! They have, between them, six out of nine million acres!

Four individuals own one sixteenth. Lord Lovat alone has 200,000 acres. The Countess of Seafield has 216,000 acres. And the Duke of Buccleuch has 500,000 acres. (*Red Paper on Scotland*, pp 262-70) Meanwhile, in the cities, working-class people fight for every inch of space, spend lifetimes struggling to keep a roof over their heads, paying the inflated rents and mortgages that are the inevitable consequence of this stranglehold over all wealth and natural resources.

There can be no serious social progress until the stranglehold is broken. Yet the nationalists have no intention of acknowledging its existence, never mind doing anything to destroy it. The nationalists want to ingratiate themselves with people of power and wealth. They want to be all things to all men. So while they make gestures towards working people, they are also at pains to underline their respectability and reliability.

This is why they support the monarchy. This is why they say nothing about the centuries-old, and still continuing, national oppression of Ireland. This is why they support massive spending on arms and other forms of repression without which their rich friends and backers couldn't entertain even a hope of survival. This is also why the SNP decline to mobilise their supporters outside the sphere of passive electoral politics. Above all they want to contain their rank and file, for fear of 'things' getting out of hand.

The SNP's anxiety to cover over class divisions goes hand in hand with dishonesty about another fundamental feature of the world in which we live. Scottish society is fused into a world-wide system of plunder and exploitation.

Jacques Maisonrouge, president of the IBM World Trade Corporation, one of the biggest multinationals, puts it this way:

'For business purposes the boundaries that separate one nation from another are no more real than the equator.... Once management understands and accepts this world economy, its view of the market place — and its planning — necessarily expands. *The world outside the home country is no longer viewed as a series of disconnected customers and prospects for its products but as an extension of a single market.*' (Extract from a speech by Maisonrouge quoted in *Global Reach: the power of the multinational corporations* by R J Barnet & R E Muller p. 14)

This world system has existed since the beginning of this century. But since the end of the Second World War it has become even more centralised. The multinational corporations are at the heart of this process. Their power is growing so fast that, according to one American authority, Professor Howard Perlmutter, two to three hundred global corporations will, by 1985, control 80 per cent of all the productive assets of the 'non Communist' world. A more conservative estimate from the US Chamber of Commerce economist J. Polk envisages that by the year 2000 a few hundred multinationals will own 54 per cent of all wealth-producing assets in the world. (Quoted *Global Reach* p. 26)

In Scotland they've already taken over. Fifty-nine per cent of workers in manufacturing are already employed by companies based outside Scotland. Three-quarters of firms with more than 5000 employees are externally controlled. Twice as much per capita is invested in Scotland by American multinationals as in Britain as a whole, with Scotland coming second only to Canada as the US multinationals' favourite staging post. (Information extracted from John Firn's study in *The Red Paper on Scotland*.)

If anything, multinational power is even more intensely developed in oil — the very industry which the nationalists expect to float the economy to a new nirvana of prosperity for all. Yet, as a number of studies of the oil industry have shown, the oil barons specialise in arousing great expectations and then ruthlessly and remorselessly crushing them.

There is no nice, respectable, reformist way of breaking this worldwide stranglehold. And there is no way of breaking it within a purely Scottish context any more than there is within a purely British context.

Socialism is internationalist or it is nothing. To the immense power and organisation of exploiters across the globe, we can and must counterpose the power and potential of the working class of the whole world.

Socialism sets out to abolish the antagonisms and divisions between the peoples of the world. Socialism means large units, closer and closer fraternal relationships between all countries and peoples. It involves a United States of Europe. It involves a Union of Soviet Republics or whatever you care to call it, and ultimately it means fully-flowered socialism itself, a United States of the World.

But ours will be *free* unions of *free* nations. They will have not a whiff or a trace of chauvinism or national oppression on them. For that is the only way we can possibly succeed in doing what has to be done.

This is why no socialist worthy of the name can even unintentionally defend the British arrangement of things or Westminster's exclusive right to form a state. We are unambiguously and without qualification for the right of self-determination for all nations and for a referendum to decide which arrangement people favour. We have nothing in common with the British nationalism of Labour MP Eric Heffer, who is wedded to the British state and who, when he talks about the unity of the working class, sees it only within a L nd's End to John O'Groats 'British' context.

But our job isn't only to fight British nationalism. Above all, we value the international unity of the working class. So we must fight for the closest possible alliance of workers irrespective of any reshaping of the frontiers of the individual states. And we must fight in the here and now.

We do not and cannot, even unintentionally, favour the Scottish employing class over the 'British' or 'English' version. We cannot vouch for any society over which any such people exercise any measure of control.

And the nationalists *do* want to split that unity which is the only thing of value Scots, English and Welsh workers have had out of the 'British arrangement'. They generally go to considerable lengths to disguise what they have in mind by way of separate Scottish unions. But, in one field, the field of trade unionism among students, the SNP has come right out into the open.

In the December 1976 issue of the SNP paper *Scots Independent* their columnist Albert Ross wrote a piece called 'No NUS is good news'. This, as the title indicates, strongly recommended the break-up of the present international organisation of Scots, English and Welsh students.

Yet students north and south of the border face common problems and would continue to do so even if the Royal High Assembly became a fully fledged Parliament. And surely it is a legitimate question to ask: 'Where next after students?' Do the SNP want to set the miners back half a century and separate them from their natural allies, their comrades in the coalfields of Yorkshire, South Wales and Kent? Do they favour a Scottish Union of Engineers?

Instead of promoting more democracy and rank and file power, the SNP wants to inject the working-class movement with yet another layer of careerists. But what we need isn't more well-paid, appointed-for-life jobs for the boys as Charlotte Square trade union bureaucrats. We need more and more rank and file power, more combine and international links with our natural allies in Liverpool and Manchester and Dublin and, indeed, in Turin, Lisbon and Lyons.

The essays in this book show the magnetic power of the working class in motion. They show how people react under a wide variety of stimuli from at home and from abroad. They show how people explode into struggle and how that struggle begins to reach out for power over society as a whole.

The essays focus mainly on the last great flourish of working-class power just over half a century ago. They contain much new material because they are concerned with a feature of history that is usually neglected and without which history would not exist — the self-activity of working men and women. Among other things the essays prove that you get what you fight for, that no-one can give you freedom. Freedom you have to take for yourself.

It is this that makes them extraordinarily relevant to our own times. There are great, even decisive, struggles coming within these islands.

In these struggles, working people will once again throw up institutions of their own making. The question is whether they are to rise or fall, whether the working class will conquer or be crushed.

A real working-class party with deep roots in the working class can make sure that workers' power does prevail. But that party must be big enough *before* the crisis comes to stand a chance of growing into a genuine mass party within the crisis.

The members of the Socialist Workers Party are doing everything in their power to build such an organisation. But the most important people for our organisation are those who are not already members.

That is why this book closes not only with an outline of the very recent struggles of the working class, but with an unashamed appeal to all those who read these pages and are inspired by them to join us without delay.

1 The People's Republic of Fife: the story of the Methil Council of Action

Laurie Flynn

How can working people run their own lives? What structures do they need to fashion to ensure that democracy is an every-day living thing and not a sham? Would workers' power really work? Or is it all a nice but impossible dream?

These are familiar questions and the answers do not come easy, tripping off the tongue. For answers have to be found in the real, living experience of working-class people.

Just over fifty years ago, workers in the coalfields of Fife, in company with other workers elsewhere, set about providing some answers to these questions. Miners, railwaymen and dockers combined to forge Councils of Action in the great strike of 1926. Arising out of the battle against the employers and the government, the Councils were weapons of agitation and propaganda, the indispensable means of prosecuting a struggle and beating off the challenge from the state.

But the Councils of Action were more than this. No sooner had they come into existence than they began to develop in a profoundly revolutionary direction. They became the means of exercising working-class power and authority over whole areas. They pointed the way *in practice* towards a new form of democracy, and a new society which would be ruled directly by those who produce the means of life. The Councils of Action were a first working drawing of workers' power in embryo. They show in rich and intoxicating detail that workers really can run their own lives and govern their own states. And they show *how* it can be done.

Next to nothing has been written about these glorious achievements of Fife miners, dockers and railwaymen and the communities of which they were a part. This is not surprising. The employing class has an enormous interest in laundering the record so that such obvious inspiration is obliterated. Yet despite the activities of such as Augustus Muir, the bought and paid for historian of the Fife Coal Company, whose 'study' of the General Strike led him to the conclusion that 'nothing untoward' or rather nothing at all had happened in the County and Kingdom of Fife in 1926, something has got through.

For example the comedian Chic Murray tells a story about the People's Republic of Fife and its Commissar Vladimir McGuffy. In a letter to Mr Murray, so the story goes, Vladimir informed him that he was a Leninist. "You know, len' us this and len' us that." This story and others like it are probably inspired by the historic events of 1926.

One of the few published references to these marvellous achievements of the common people came in Emile Burn's book *Trades Councils in Action*. This briefly gave some indication of the strength of organisation thrown up in Methil during the great strike.

'For its courier service the (Methil) Council had three motor cars, 100 motor cycles and as many ordinary bicycles as were necessary. These worked under the information committee, covering the whole of Fife, bringing in reports, taking out information, and carrying speakers who were everywhere in demand. Speakers went as far north as Perth; a panel of 30 speakers was drawn up (they went in threes: a miner, a railwayman, a docker) and speakers' notes were issued by the propaganda committee. A daily news bulletin was duplicated. There were daily meetings and demonstrations.'

But the Methil Council did far more than this. It became a real power in the land much more by doing things than saying them or causing them to be said.

Fife was one of the few areas in the country where, before May 1926, there were conscious and deliberate preparations for the coming struggle. Early in April 1926, Lochgelly Trades Council, strongly influenced by the revolutionary socialists of the Communist Party, called a conference to set up a Central Committee of Action for Fife, Kinross and Clackmannan. The meeting also called on other local trades councils to set up councils of action. On 22 April the Methil Trades and Labour Council met to discuss the possibilities and talk about a workers' defence corps. And even before this in speeches, leaflets and pit-papers, the message of practical unity was being got across.

By contrast with the national leaders of the official movement, the minority of politically conscious activists in the Fife coalfield were doing everything they could to make ready for the struggle ahead. But they were only a small minority, albeit one with an unshakeable faith in the capacity of the working class. So when they called a meeting at Denbeath Bridge on the Sunday just before the General Strike, it had to be cancelled for lack of attendance. The following Sunday, when the strike was on, they held another meeting. The turn-out was massive.

Struggle had unlocked the creative capacities of the masses. Those who had been the most disparaging of their own and other people's ability to run their own lives, changed out of all recognition.

They began to prove in practice that they could control their own destinies. Under the harsh realities of capitalism, they might decline to dream. After all, dreaming is painful. It makes slavery even less bearable. But given the chance to realise a dream, to prove the truth, people rose like lions.

This is how John McArthur, chairman of the Methil Council of Action in 1926, recalls that rising today:

'When the strike took place the first thing to get going was organisation. Our slogans locally were: "All power to the councils of action". We said each organisation had to give up power to the Council of Action. There was no disagreement.

'We were in fact the only people around who said what people should do. So the workers accepted our leadership. There hadn't been a general strike before. So when it took place we were the undoubted leadership of it. Adamson, MP and general secretary of the Old Union of Miners, from which we had broken away into the Reform Union, was just ignored.

'The Co-op small hall was given to us as headquarters. The duplicator belonging to the group of us who published the Communist pit paper *The Spark* was handed over for the use of the council. Davie Proudfoot, checkweigher at the Wellesley pit in whose name *The Spark* was published, became the organisational convener. He was in truth a genius, though with some limitations. He worked best when the ideas were his own rather than other people's. And, of course, he didn't have all the best ideas.

'And so as he suggested it, it was drawn up. His diagram for the Methil Council of Action is still in existence. We drew up a speaker's panel. It was agreed that no miner would go out alone. Every meeting was to be addressed by a group representing miners, dockers and railwaymen. It was group leadership we were out to forge. We set up a committee to raise money. There was a cycle corps for communications. This was so successful that the East Fife Motor Cycle Club volunteered en bloc to help us. We had a committee to issue permits allowing some people to move goods or lorries.

'When the strike took place, there were no problems about blacklegging here. The only problem was the organisations that hadn't been ordered out. They were clamouring to come out and in most cases out they came. While there were no blacklegs here we still made as much propaganda as possible for a defence corps. We ended up with what is now recognised as the most developed one in Britain.

'This issue exploded in Methil. We were up speaking at the corner not far from where I live now. The news was brought that there had been a baton charge on the pickets. By the time we got there we found three lads had been arrested and were in the cells.

'At that time this housing scheme we live on now was just being built. So there was plenty of material around. And by the time we arrived the women were chasing the police out of it for dear life. "Let's get after them. Let's get the laddies out," was the cry.

'After a lot of persuading, we got the people down to the strike headquarters for a hastily summoned meeting. I chaired it and Davie Proudfoot had to outline the position of the Council of Action. He went on about the Workers' Defence Corps we were after. He talked about support for an International Class War Prisoners Aid to pay for lawyers and the like. Those were the two things we hammered at the meeting. After a lot of argument we won the day.

'Then, with the meeting concluded, Proudfoot called on the audience to line up as follows. He asked all the men with military experience to go to one side of the hall. Then he asked those without any to go to the other.

'Next he asked for everyone with a stripe to come to the front. Each of them was put in charge of ten privates and each private was put in charge of ten of the people without military experience. We didn't run to any officers. But we did have one sergeant of the Black Watch. He became the commander of the Methil Workers' Defence Corps.

'The strongest demand was to march up the road and force release of the arrested lads. We were against that and we were losing. We'd never have won if the father of one of the boys hadn't stood up. "You can't have a war without some casualties. It's just unfortunate that my son is one of the first." But for that we'd have lost.

'We had 600 volunteers for the Workers' Defence Corps. The pickets were marching up the road in hard hats and pit boots. By this time the police had been reinforced with bus load after bus load of men. The chief picket dropped off enough men to block off every approach road and then held the balance of our men in reserve. He had his men posted up the road ready to tell him whenever a lorry was coming. They went out by cycle with a ball of thread unwinding as they went. Each was attached to one of his fingers and if he felt a tug he knew that a lorry or something was coming.

'So this beer lorry came. We took every single barrel off it and let them run out in front of the police. They gave us no trouble at all. Everyone looked to the Council of Action. Its authority was unquestioned. If anyone had a problem they came to us and the Council solved it.

'When the strike was called off, after nine days of growing power and organisation, we couldn't believe it. We were stunned. There was no reason. Each day it went on we had gained in confidence. We had new and marvellous experiences in the struggle. We had mass meetings every night, wonderful meetings five and six thousand strong. We were full of vim, full of go. We were spreading out, too, sending speakers to Perth and other places.

'In this area, there was a remarkable feeling of confidence and strength, an awareness of what we were accomplishing. After the strike was off the railmen and the dockers simply would not go back. And then the miners decided to fight on. We were accustomed to long drawn-out struggles, not least here in Fife. Then, because we had no money, it was vital to organise communal feeding. The Council of Action set up soup kitchens and divided the whole area up.

'Where we could find a house with a big washing boiler we would use that for making the soup. Where we couldn't we would build a big unit installing our own water, gas and electricity. Then in each area we would organise a kitchen committee elected by popular vote. Each committee had to have a kitchen convener and assistant convener.

'We had a roll call of all the people who were due to come for their food. And it was understood that everyone getting food had to take their turn at the toil so that the operation wasn't based on ones and twos. There wasn't the slightest hint of an objection. Everyone understood that it was fair and because it was fair they did their turn.

'We organised everyone to apply for public assistance to the Parish Council offices. There was about a half mile of a queue. When the queue was established we went in to see the Parish Council Chairman and said to him: "How are you going to handle this? You can't cope." "What have you got in mind," he replied. We quickly came to the point. "We'll do it." So the Parish Council made its payments, not to individuals but straight to the committee. We would go to the Co-op and place our orders. We told them that the Parish Council was paying. The bill came to the kitchen conveners.   They turned it over to the central kitchen committee and they paid it.

'We had an organisation to go round the gardens getting whatever produce there was there. We had people out round the farmers begging, borrowing or stealing tatties and the rest. Some responded very well. Fish merchants gave us box after box of kippers. From bakers we had rolls for the morning. We were able to provide three meals daily, more than people got in "normal" times.

'We were blessed with good weather. But the struggle went longer than we expected and this raised problems. People were in difficulty with shoes. So we got amateur shoe repairers to set up shop. It was their strike activity to repair shoes. You just brought your shoes to the kitchen convener and they brought them in. We had haircutting organised too. We met all those problems all right. But then, with November coming in, people needed pennies for the gas meter. The committee allocated the money.

'The right wing miners' group led by Adamson came under a lot of pressure when it came to feeding the schoolchildren. They had to do something. So when the money came from the Russian miners it was sent through the Miners Federation of Great Britain to them. It was laughable. Here was this man who ranted on about "Reds" being agents of a foreign power giving out Russian money.

'Throughout the whole struggle, the organisation of women was emphasised. In the United Mineworkers of Scotland that emerged after the strike when the reactionaries refused to accept our victory in elections to various official positions, we had a UMS Women's Guild for each branch. Women had the right to attend all the branch meetings and to appoint one delegate to sit on the branch committee.

'We had the self-government of the workers then. It was there. It actually existed. When I look back at the power and organisation we had then and I hear about all the progress we are supposed to have made, I know it's just not true.

'The roots of it all came in the days when we were campaigning against the Old Union. We were forced to collect dues door to door. And what a good thing that was for us. Each committee man had a number of streets to cover. He was in contact with the women. He didn't deal only with pit problems but increasingly with problems affecting the whole community, with every area of people's lives. That was the seedbed of it all.

'And what fruit it bore. When the crisis came, our principal opponent on the Trades and Labour Council became one of its toughest leaders. He was in charge of the issuing of permits. He was as solid as a brick wall during the crisis. He really flowered and developed. His name was Harry Ewing. I saw that he had died, aged 94, recently. Which leaves only me to tell of this great period in the history of the working class in Scotland.'

These remarkable events were paralleled in Lochgelly and Cowdenbeath and other places. At the height of the struggle, whole tracts of Fife were completely under the control of the Councils of Action. Police were either frightened to enter an area or, where they kept a presence, were unable or unwilling to do anything.

So where the workers had their own defence corps, there was less violence, not more. For the police and other agents of the state are far less anxious to attack those with the means of defending themselves, as Mr McArthur has testified:

'I remember going down to the strike headquarters when the first company (of the defence corps) were going to resume the picketing and as they came up with their sergeant in front, he shouted "Eyes left".

'You could see their arms swinging rigidly because they were concealing pokers, hammers etc. The picket took up its post on the road.... In spite of the fact that there was a big contingent of police they stopped every vehicle that came along. It was a marvellous display of organised, disciplined unity.

(Quoted in *The General Strike,* edited Skelley, p. 158.)

The Cowdenbeath miners' leader Bob Selkirk underlines the truly democratic nature of this organisation in his pamphlet *Life of a Worker*:

'....unity did not mean there were not differences of opinion. On day-to-day tactics there were "rights" and "lefts". For example at one meeting of the Cowdenbeath Trades Council, the subject under discussion was "police attacks on pickets". I put the case for pickets carrying pick shafts, arguing that the police would not attack strong pickets if they knew the pickets were armed with pick shafts. 'This was too much for the chairman, who rushed from the platform towards me shouting "I'll shove a pick shaft down your throat if ye try to tell me that pickets armed with pick shafts are peaceful pickets."'

In embryo this was a more straight forward and honest democracy than that available in any parliamentary debating chamber — wherever it might be located. For this is working-class self-government, or a first tender shoot of it. This form of democracy doesn't degenerate into deceptions because the delegates themselves have to work, have to execute their own decisions; and because they account on a day-by-day, hour-by-hour basis to the rank and file.

Concluding the short interview which he gave me, John McArthur was clear about what had been done. 'In these great struggles we had established, we ourselves had made the means whereby we could have run our own lives. We had it in our hands, it actually existed.'

But in full stride, it was cut down by the union leaders. Frightened at the spectre of rank and file power mushrooming throughout Scotland, Wales and England, the official leaders of the movement opted for the certainties of the present system of society — which assured their privileged position — and called off the General Strike.

Faced with this awful betrayal, the Councils of Action and other working-class bodies fought a rearguard action to prevent victimisations and reprisals on a most massive scale. But it was too late to try to carry on and develop the General Strike from below, even though the strike was still growing when it was betrayed.

The Councils of Action weren't federated or coordinated enough to do the necessary job. And the council members were themselves stunned by the betrayal. They could have been forewarned. They should have been forewarned.But most of the top leadership of the party to which the best of them all belonged had gone soft on the alleged virtues of left-wing union leaders and therefore the Communist Party did not prepare for betrayal.

That betrayal by bureaucrats, left as well as right, is one major lesson of the General Strike. But the other, just as important, is the amazing capacity of working-class people for struggle and for self-emancipation.

John McArthur is rightly proud of what was achieved in Fife during the General Strike. But he has been at pains to point out the multitude of local, national and international influences that operated on the area. It is also clear from what he says that for much of the time in the run-up to the high point of 1926 the job of the socialist was to stay with the struggle at its every level. It was essential to work patiently to increase the self-confidence and self-activity of ordinary working people. And throughout it was essential to keep in front of yourself the vision of what can be won when the struggle does explode. Otherwise tremendous opportunities would be passed up when, for a few days or weeks, they presented themselves.

In 1924 and 1925 there must have been some temptation not to do this. Instead you could look back on the none-too-distant past and feel overshadowed by it. But the uncompromising revolutionaries held firm in their belief that the struggle would explode anew. They took as raw material what had happened in 1921 at Bowhill when miners printed their own money, or at Thornton's strategic junction when they captured the station and evaded arrest by marching home along the railway line. And they tried to see how their activities could help to create a bridge between the struggle and working-class power.

They spoke at meetings in halls and in streets arguing the case for socialism. They produced pit papers and bulletins which tackled the most complicated political questions of the day in a genuinely popular and enthusing way. These publications also took up the economic and safety issues again and again and tried to organise and give a lead on them.

Their purpose was to expand the confidence and creativity of the working class, and to find ways in the hurly-burly of real life to give them organised expression. They were revolutionary, not resolutionary, socialists.

They saw the rank and file power that they so passionately believed in flower and briefly flourish. They also saw it cut down. After it was laid low in 1926, 'normality' was quickly restored. 'Normality' meant submission to the boss, wage cuts, lousy, unsafe and downright deadly conditions, unemployment and, before long, fascism and war.

In a 1932 circular from the right-wing Fife, Kinross and Clackmannan Miners Union our old friend W Adamson set out in some detail what the defeat and the ensuing crisis meant for the miners:

> 'Men off sick or suffering from industrial accidents and diseases were being told their places had been filled when they tried to resume work. Men were being refused work because they didn't live in company houses — the company had to get its rents as well as its profits. And men were accepting individual wage reductions and were too frightened to report them to the union for fear that they would be victimised.'

(Secretary's circular, 23 November 1932)

There was — and is — an alternative to this rotten society which we can see everywhere around us today. That alternative is to be found in working-class independence and working-class self-government. If humanity is to have a half decent future and begin constructing a truly human history free of exploitation and misery, it will be done through institutions of workers' power exactly like Methil's Council of Action.

Footnote: Ian MacDougall, secretary of the Scottish Labour History Society, has done more than any one to ensure that this rich heritage of struggle is retained. He has tape-recorded many hours of John McArthur's memories and reminiscences. A hint of what the resulting manuscript must contain is given in at least two places – in Ian MacDougall's essay in **The General Strike** edited by Jeffrey Skelley and published by Lawrence and Wishart; and in his short research report in **Oral History**, Volume Two, Number One (Spring 1974). It is to be hoped that his manuscript is published sooner rather than later. The book will undoubtedly be one of the most important publications on working-class history in Scotland for many years.

2 We shall not be removed
Ann and Vincent Flynn

If respect for our Parliamentary system has patently withered, it is because it has failed the needs of the people; it has failed to provide the people's simplest basic needs: homes, food, work, and proper medical care.

The failure is chronic and endemic. The old medicines with the new labels neither cure nor deceive the sufferers. Will the years ahead be those when the patient finally rejects the medicine? We shall see. But it will help if we take a look at 1915, when such a crisis in the people's needs made that year a very special one, of the greatest import-ance in the history of the working class.

The symptoms of the breakdown in both periods are the same: food prices doubled, fuel beyond the reach of many, a famine in hous-ing. But 1915 was the year when the phenomenal struggles of the 'Rent Strikers', most of whom were unpoliticised, voteless women, wrested from an unwilling government an Act to restrict the greed of the pro-perty owners. That restriction, won by the street-to-street fighting action of the working class, is still embodied in the Rent Restriction Act.

Where did the trouble begin? Who started the strikes? How were they organised? Who were the leaders? For answers to these questions we look to the orthodox social historians in vain. Newspaper and other reports tend to suggest that the rent strike struggles were brief and spas-modic, confined within a few months of 1915. Not so. It was a long and bitter fight which spanned the years 1911 to 1920, with a critical testing time in 1915. It was no accident that Scotland offered the strongest resistance to the rapacity of the landlords and their agents and that Glasgow, a city savaged by the Industrial Revolution, should be its launching pad. But the rent strikes spread nationwide because the greed of property owners and the harshness of the Munitions Acts of a war-time government combined to spark off the fires of discontent which raged in all the munitions areas throughout Britain, as well as in some rural areas such as Wiltshire and, of course, the mining communities. First, let us look at the historical background.

Under the impact of the Industrial Revolution, Glasgow expanded rapidly. Two other factors contributed to its congestion: first was an influx of Highlanders driven from ancestral lands by clan chiefs who preferred the cries of sheep to the calls of kin; then came a steady stream of previously dispossessed Irish peasants fleeing from famine. Since both groups were poor, no speculative builder saw profit in their presence, so they had to crowd into already densely populated areas of the city. For many landlords these developments offered opportunities for gain with little effort. Properties were sub-divided; individual rooms in a small family house each became the home of a single family. It is impossible to exaggerate the pressure put upon living space. St. Mungo's 'dear green place' had become for thousands of honest, decent people a drear, grim place. Here is a description of the living conditions of the Glasgow poor towards the end of the nineteenth century, given to the Royal Commission on the Housing of the Industrial Population of Scotland by Glasgow's Medical Officer of Health at the time, Dr J B Russell:

'Figures are beyond the reach of sentiment and if they are sensational, it is only because of their terrible undisguised truthfulness. You must not think of the inmates of those small houses as families in the ordinary sense of the term. No less than 14 per cent of one-roomed houses and 27 per cent of two-roomed contain lodgers — strange men and women mixed up with husbands and wives and children, within the four walls of small rooms. Nor must I permit you in noting down the same average of fully three inmates in each of these one-apartment houses to remain ignorant of the fact that there are thousands of these houses which contain five, six, and seven inmates, and hundreds which are inhabited by from eight up even to thirteen. Percentages, though an accurate, are but a feeble mode of expression for such facts regarding men and women like ourselves. I have told you that in 1881 the population of Glasgow was 511,520 persons and that of those 25 per cent lived in one-room and 45 per cent in two-roomed houses. But what does that mean? It means that 126,000 persons *live* (his italics) in these one-roomed and 228,000 in these two-roomed houses. But is that all I can say? I might throw down that statement before you and ask you to imagine yourselves, with all your appetites and passions, your bodily necessities and functions, your feelings of modesty, your sense of propriety, your births, your deaths, your children — in short your *lives* in the whole round of their relationships with the seen and the unseen, suddenly shrivelled and shrunk into such conditions of space. I might ask you, I do ask you, to consider and honestly confess what would be the result to you.

But I would fain do more. Generalities are so feeble. Yet how can I speak to you decently of details? Where can I find language in which to clothe the facts of these poor people's lives and still be tolerable?'

It is true to say that for these 'homes' fit only for heroes, the people paid two rents: the weekly cash rent and a life rent — that is to say they paid with their lives. Between the middle-class residential area of Pollockshields and Blackfriars, the most congested slum in Europe, the distance was two miles. But the health figures were life-miles apart. The respective figures per thousand were: death rate, 10.3 and 29.2; TB 1.4 and 3.9; infant mortality, 27 and 178. In the face of such figures certain members of the City Council solemnly affirmed that the difference was due to climatic variation. But they did effect some changes. Blackfriars, the most congested slum in Europe, disappeared into Gorbals, the best known slum in the western world. And in the official language the dreaded word Tuberculosis was abandoned for the term Phthisis. Thus Latin learning paid back its debt to Greek. Meanwhile the people perished.

Over the years the housing stock increased, but not sufficiently to eliminate the overcrowding, although it was reduced from the terrible levels shown by Dr Russell. The old, small sub-divided houses were replaced, or more often supplemented, by huge fortress-like tenement blocks of separate one-roomed (single ends) and two-roomed (double ends or but and ben) tenement flats, their front doors opening off a common stair, which the tenants took it in turns to wash and keep clean. There was a water closet on each half landing. In some older tenements, there was a communal water supply provided by a tap in the back court or on the half landing between ground and first floor. In the more modern flats there was a black, cast-iron sink with one cold-water tap (the 'jaw box' so dear to the heart of generations of Glasgow comedians).

Along an interior wall of the flat there was often one, sometimes two, bed recesses, which the housewife kept curtained for privacy and also for decorative display. Beside the bed usually stood a plain deal chair, which served the small children and often the small wives as a mounting block to get into the fairly high bed. The curtains had other uses besides shielding sleeping children from the light; they afforded the only privacy available to wives and daughters as they stripped and changed and attended to their bodily needs. Under the beds were stored baskets and baths and other household items not in constant use. In a cupboard under the sink was usually kept a garbage pail whose contents were emptied regularly into an ashpit in the back court of the tenement. For night use there might also be a chamber pot, which was also kept under the sink, discreetly covered, yet whose presence at times soured the air.

Nailed to the front doors of many of the older tenement flats was a round cast-iron disc bearing a number embossed on its face, say, 2½ or 3. The explanation of this mystery is simple. About 1900 a survey of accommodation had been carried out by the public health authority. The figures meant that the accommodation was sufficient for only two and a half or three persons, as the case might be. No, there is no mistake. The figure given is two and a half. In this way the tenant was branded as the offender in the many cases of overcrowding thus established, although that was not necessarily the intention of the scheme's devisers. Another hazard was added to people's lives. The tenant who complained about the lack of essential repairs could and did have pointed out to him his own violation of the law in overcrowding domestic premises. All except the boldest spirits were silenced and houses fell into ever greater disrepair.

With the outbreak of war all house-building ceased, leaving many more miserably aware of their discomforts and dangers as inhabitants of Britain's most overcrowded area than proud of the dubious distinction of living in the second city of the Empire. The general death rate that year was 16.6 per thousand. In the elegant west-end district of Kelvinside it was only 8.7, while in Broomielaw, part of Glasgow's dockland, it was 24.3! For the infant population, Broomielaw and Blackfriars, were an express-train journey to Paradise. Unemployment was added to other troubles for many because of lay-offs in the service trades. On the other hand, engineering and shipbuilding expanded, bringing more workers to the city and adding further pressures to housing demand. Some men brought from Woolwich Arsenal refused to live in the tenement houses offered them. Rents were rising, prices were rising. Wages were effectively controlled by the operation of the Munitions Acts, which prevented those affected from leaving their employment without their employer's permission.

Just before the outbreak of war, the engineers had lodged a wage claim with their employers for an extra 2d an hour. The employers' delaying tactics, followed by an offer of one halfpenny an hour, did nothing to sweeten industrial relations. And the knowledge that 'patriots' were piling up fortunes soured the atmosphere further. In the minds of a growing number, the vague longings of the poor were being transformed into the determined demands of a class. Relationships were changing because an awareness of the nature of those relationships, thanks to the efforts of John Maclean and others, was growing among workers. The year 1915 ushered in a period of determined opposition to employers and landlords.

That year in Glasgow the annual May Day demonstration, in the words of one local paper, *Partick and Maryhill Press*, "was organised on a larger scale than on any previous occasion. Over 165 Labour and Socialist organisations took part....and Glasgow Green was crowded with thousands of spectators. There were 12 platforms. Among those represented were those of the Socialist and Labour Party, Internationalism, Glasgow Housing Committee, the Anarchist Group, Socialist Children's School, and Women Trade Unionists. One platform was devoted to the propaganda work of the Glasgow Housing Committee, and addresses were delivered by Councillors George Kerr, Izett and Wheatley (later Minister of Health in the first Labour Government). Councillor Kerr said that housing reform was more urgently required in Glasgow today than ever before. Rents were going up with greater rapidity than in normal times. Landlords had made up their minds that in existing conditions there was an opportunity to exploit....and they were exploiting the opportunity as much as they could. The only way the citizens could counteract this was to adopt the principles and policy of the Labour Party in the Town Council — that no interest should be paid on capital used to build houses. Councillor Wheatley said that what they wanted to do first was to educate the workers to realise that as they created the best they were entitled to the best. They would never get the best if they begged for it. They would have to work out their own salvation by binding themselves together and by not permitting political or religious differences to separate them.'

Since 1905 Wheatley, who, as an Irish immigrant and a coalminer, had bitter experience of overcrowded slum housing, had devoted himself to developing plans for clearing the slums. His plan, summed up in the slogan '£8 Cottages', was to build municipal houses using interest-free capital borrowed from the considerable surpluses produced annually by Glasgow's excellent public transport. His scheme caught the imagination and fuelled the desperate dreams of many trapped in the city's terrible housing, which might have been conjured up by a Hogarth in a moment of madness and despair. Two organisations which carried on constant propaganda for Wheatley's plan were Glasgow Women's Housing Association and Glasgow Labour Party Housing Committee.

The first rent strike took place in the Govan district of Glasgow in May, 1915. The firm of estate agents which factored 250 tenement dwellings there informed the tenants individually that with effect from 28 May their rents were to be increased by sums ranging from 12 shillings to 24 shillings per annum. This was the second increase since the outbreak of war. Some of the affected tenants canvassed their neighbours, the Govan District of the Women's Housing Association held a protest meeting, and immediately other groups such as the Labour Representation Committee (Govan Branch) joined forces with the tenants. The main plan of campaign was to offer the ordinary rent, but refuse to pay the proposed increase. This plan was faithfully carried out: the tenants duly offered the rent without the increase demanded; the factor refused the sums offered. It was to be a long time before Messrs Neilson again collected rents in those particular tenements.

Their efforts baulked, the factors decided to frighten their tenants into submission. A rumour was spread to the effect that one of the big engineering firms in the area, Messrs Harland and Wolff Ltd, had requested the factors to find 100 to 150 houses for additional workers they proposed to bring into the area. Fortunately, two women members of the Tenants' Defence Committee had the good sense to write Harland & Wolff to confirm the story. The reply of the firm's managing director, Mr John Dickinson, which was published in *Forward* on 5 June, must be one of the rare examples of publicly expressed disagreement between members of the property-owning and employing class. Not only did Dickinson deny having sought Messrs Neilson's assistance to find houses then or being likely to do so in the future, he went on to say: 'We are very pleased to hear that the tenants of the Govan district purpose refusing to pay the increased rents, and we sympathise entirely with them. We trust that the legislature will intervene to annul all the increases which have recently taken place and to prevent any further increases, as it seems to us there is absolutely no justification for them.' No doubt this engineering employer was not the complete altruist; no doubt he was simply seeking to keep the peace among his own workers, some of whom were certainly the husbands or sons of the women rent strikers. The fact remains that he need not have shown his partisanship so plainly. We greatly doubt that such a letter would be written today.

Having taken the first step, the women began to organise themselves for what was to prove a long struggle, whose echoes were to resound in every ordnance factory in Britain, in many town and county councils, and in Parliament itself. Meetings were organised at the gates of the big engineering and shipbuilding yards in the area — Fairfield, Stephens, Harland and Wolff. In that way and also through the speeches of most of the Glasgow ILP councillors, the Clyde Workers' Committee collectively and individually, and John Maclean, who from the first clearly saw and preached its significance, Glasgow got news of the Govan rent strike.

Forward, edited by Tom Johnston, and John Maclean's *Vanguard* carried full reports and gave sympathetic encouragement, but Glasgow's capitalist newspapers managed to resist their oft insisted duty to inform. Without detracting in any way from the efforts of those mentioned, it is essential to understand the nature and size of the contribution made by ordinary housewives, those unknown soldiers who guarded the hearths and homes of others as well as withstanding threats to their own. Occasionally a name appears, such as that of Mrs Ferguson or Mrs Barbour, who jointly wrote the letter which elicited the reply from Harland & Wolff referred to above and who jointly helped in organising defences against surprise visits by Sheriff's officers (bailiffs) as well as addressing meetings in the city. There was also Mrs Helen Crawfurd, the wife of a Free Church minister, a suffragette who had suffered imprisonment, had several times gone on hunger strike, and who, according to Willie Gallacher in *Revolt on the Clyde*, was fearless and impervious to police intimidation.

Across the narrow waters of River Clyde opposite Govan, on the north bank lies the busy working-class district of Partick. Although there were several engineering works and shipyards in Partick and further west, each morning thousands of men and a growing number of women crossed the river to work. They brought back the news of the stirring events in Govan. They, too, had had their rents increased and their landlords and the factors were demanding more and threatening tenants with eviction. Once again the people organised themselves and refused to pay the increases. The rapacity and cruelty of the house factors is equalled only by the fighting spirit of the tenants.

It is appropriate at this point to say something about the defence strategy of the women. The first need was an early warning system to alert the strikers to approching danger. The women in each tenement close set a guard on a rota system. Often enough this job would be done by girls, who had learned patience and vigilance in the course of looking after younger brothers and sisters. The warden on duty had a handbell, a racket such as used to be favoured by football fans, a tin basin and spoon — anything that would make enough noise to warn of the approach of a stranger or any other apprehended danger. Summoned by the noise, the housewives would hasten to the scene, armed for combat. The favourite weapons were small bags filled with pease-meal, dry flour or whiting. The Sheriff's officers did not relish assaults with such weapons. In addition, tenants were organised into street groups, which liaised with local Tenants' Defence Leagues, Working Women's Associations, the Trades Council, the Clyde Workers' Committee and the ILP councillors. By these means information could be passed on quickly, masses of people brought to a central point for a meeting or a march through a locality or to the city centre. There were many such.

The factors continued their efforts to raise rents and to evict those who refused to pay, regardless of circumstances. One man who refused to pay the higher rent and refused also to quit his house was Andrew Hood, who later became Lord Provost of Glasgow and was the first of a very few Labour provosts who refused to accept the knighthood which goes automatically to the holder of that office. On the day he was due to be evicted, a Saturday, his brother, a wounded soldier, was lying ill in Andrew Hood's house. A crowd gathered to repel the Sheriff's officer, who wisely decided to absent himself. On the same day, also in Partick, a 70-year old pensioner living alone was due to be evicted on a warrant issued by Sheriff Thomson for refusing to pay a rent increase. The old man barricaded himself in his tiny tenement flat and a large crowd gathered outside in his support, making his 'castle' impregnable. Again no official showed face, but the stories of these and other cases spread throughout the yards and engineering shops, causing considerable hardening of feeling against landlords, their factors and the authorities in general.

Perhaps one of the strangest cases of all occured in Partick. A family which had come to move into an emptied house was met by a

Postcard souvenir of the General Strike
shows Fife miners' leader John Bird in
Council of Action 'uniform'

GENERAL STRIKE

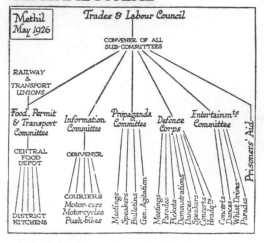

The degree of organisation in Methil is shown in this contemporary plan.

Overturning one of the scab-operated Glasgow buses during the General Strike.

Thirteen dockers were given fourteen days hard labour for picketing during the General Strike. This newspaper photograph shows them being led to prison under police guard.

Meanwhile running a soup kitchen (like this one in Hyde Park) provided passing amusement for the bored rich. Down there on a visit was Lady Mountbatten, on the far right in the photograph.

GENERAL STRIKE

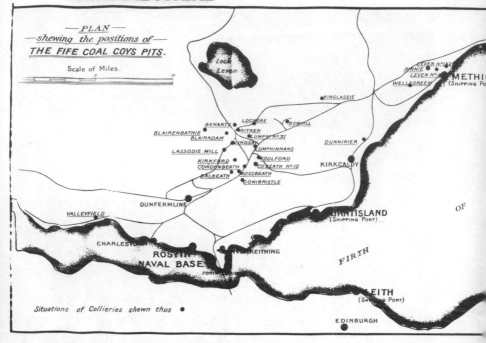

— PLAN —
shewing the positions of
THE FIFE COAL COYS PITS.

Scale of Miles.

Loch Leven

LEVEN Nº 42?
PIRNIE
LEVEN Nº
WELLSGREEN
METHI
(SHIPPING Po

KINGLASSIE

BENARTY
LOCHORE
BOWHILL
BLAIRENBATHIE
AITKEN
BLAIRADAM
LUMPHY Nº XI
LINDSAY
LASSODIE MILL
LUMPHINNANS
DUNNIKIER
KIRKFORD
FOULFORD
KIRKCALDY
COWDENBEATH
COWBEATH Nº 10
DALBEATH
MOSSBEATH
DONIBRISTLE

DUNFERMLINE

VALLEYFIELD

RNTISLAND
(SHIPPING PORT)

OF

CHARLESTOWN
ROSYTH
NAVAL BASE
NVERKEITHING

FIRTH

LEITH
(SHIPPING PORT)

Situations of Collieries shewn thus •

EDINBURGH

The O.M.S. is neither Political nor aggressive. In the event of a general strike, the members volunteer to assist the Government of the day, to the best of their ability, in the maintenance of essential Public Services of Food, Heat, Light, Transport, Sanitation etc.

Owing to the amount of unrest in the Country, the necessity for this Organisation must be apparent to all loyal Citizens.

Membership.

Those wishing to become Members can do so under one of the five classes set out on the opposite page.

Place an X against the class to which you consider yourself most suited.

Special Qualifications.

It would be of great assistance to the Secretary if details of any special qualifications were given on page 4.

Finance.

It is essential to have funds for any organisation, and those willing to contribute any sum, however small, are asked to fill in the form overleaf, but it must be understood that there is no entrance fee and that any contribution is quite voluntary.

JOIN NOW.

This page to be retained.

Please complete this page and page 4.

CLASSES.

(a) Age limit 45. To be sworn in, if required, as Special Constables to work under the Police Authorities.

(b) Those with a knowledge of work in connection with :—

Railways, Trams, Buses, Electrical Power, Gas, Water and Public Health Services.

(State your special qualifications on page 4).

(c) (1). Those who will volunteer to drive motor vans, lorries or horse drawn vehicles.

(State type of vehicle to which you are accustomed, and whether able to do own running repairs, on page 4).

(2) Those willing to handle food-stuffs and other commodities in bulk.

(State your special qualifications on page 4).

(d) Those who will undertake Messenger duties and who are able to drive cars or motor-cycles, etc.

(State your qualifications on page 4).

(e) For members who do not enrol for classes (a), (b), (c) or (d), but who are willing to assist in clerical work, canteens, hospitals, etc., or in recruiting members for the O.M.S.

Women are eligible for this class, but in no circumstances will they be employed in places where there is any danger of rough handling.

(State your qualifications on page 4).

The Fife coalfield prior to 1914.

A recruitment leaflet for the strike-breaking organisation OMS, issued prior to the General Strike.

RENT STRIKE

A tenants' demonstration in Partick against threatened evictions

Women and children
marched from
St Enoch's Square to
the Glasgow City
Chambers.

WOMEN v LANDLORDS

FORTY HOURS STRIKE

Troops were brought in from outside Glasgow, because it was feared that local troops might support the strikers.

On Bloody Friday, 31 January 1919, police wielding batons attacked part of the 30,000 strong demonstration in George Square, 'to let through a tram'.

Working conditions in
West of Scotland
foundries have changed
very little; forty years
separate these two
photographs. The first
is of Barrowfield
Foundry in the early
1930s; the second in
Chapel Street, Airdrie,
was taken in 1971.

While thousands of shipyard workers were unemployed in the 1920s, some found work, as for example those pictured opposite in Fairfield's Yard, building the TSS Montrose. As if to mock the poverty of those thrown out of work, others were engaged on fitting out the Montrose with opulent elaboration like the dining room pictured above.

Opposite: Transport and General members picket the Joe Coral betting shop chain in the campaign for union recognition (October 1974). Running down the shipbuilding industry: a crane at Govan Shipbuilders is being dismantled.

Two solutions to the problem of housing the workers in Glasgow. Leave them where they are in the slums, or tidy them away in Red Road Flats, the tallest blocks in Europe.

Glasgow Trades Council demonstration against the use of strikebreaking troops in the 1975 dust-cart drivers' strike.

hostile crowd of women, who suspected that the prospective tenants had agreed to pay the higher rent demanded by the factor, which had been refused by the previous tenant, a policeman, who had vacated the house rather than fight. The situation became menacing and the police at the station nearby were alerted. The man in charge there sent two policemen round to 'restore order', one of whom was the man who had quit the house rather than pay the factor's increased impost. This cunning ruse failed; the prospective tenants withdrew under police escort.

The struggle was not without its humorous interludes. A crowd of women who had gathered to prevent the eviction of a neighbour were joined by two soldiers who happened to be passing by. Also in the crowd was a man wearing a bowler hat. Now on a weekday in Glasgow a bowler-hatted man in a working-class district in those days could only be a shipyard foreman on the loose, a house factor or a Sheriff's officer. Entering into the spirit of things, the soldiers asked the bowler hat to advance and be recognised. The stranger made no response, and when he refused a second request to identify himself, the soldiers each took an elbow, lifted the man off his feet, carried him into the tenement back court, and deposited him in the common ashpit, which is a feature (often malodorous) of Glasgow tenement life. Later, the man denied having any connexion with Sheriff's officers, a breed of men deservedly always held in bad odour.

Throughout the months of strife there were many street demonstrations and public meetings. These were lively, colourful, good natured. But their firmness was expressed by Helen Crawfurd. She insisted that the fight was essential; that it was a woman's fight; that all those taking part in the struggle were showing their solidarity. They were asking not for mercy, not for charity; they were asking for justice. When the Government had brought in its moratorium at the beginning of the war they could have made it illegal for factors to increase rents and for bondholders to raise the rate of interest on their bonds. She respected all law that was just and fair but she did not ask them to respect the law which allowed increases in rents to be enforced at that time.

News of the rent strikes began to filter through. People in other areas organised resistance to their landlords. The miners in West Calder, some 18 miles from Edinburgh, struck work when the coal-owners sought to raise the rents of their tied houses. A few days of action brought complete victory. Resistance spread. It is interesting to mark on a map the places that were affected in one way or another by developments. As resistance to the landlord demands spread, Government concern increased. The Ministry of Munitions, anxious to avoid work stoppages, and also under the necessity to find housing accommodation for the increasing number of munition workers and their families drafted into the already crowded urban areas, also showed increasing interest. Glasgow and Dundee, Cardiff and Coventry, Birmingham and Belfast, London, Liverpool, all the towns and cities were in the grip of a housing famine. In Glasgow, derelict properties were re-opened, minimum repairs done, and tenants installed. (The writers know of one such property, a derelict backland, i.e. a tenement built on land enclosed by other tenements and reached down a narrow passage, which was always referred to by everybody except the shamed unfortunates who lived there as the 'scabby back'.) By such means as well as rent increases the rapacious landlords and their factors pursued wealth behind a smoke-screen of newspaper talk of hardship.

The driven people, working long and hard for wages kept low by the Munitions of War Act, which tied them to their jobs and forbade strikes, were learning bitter lessons. The price of food had risen sharply. Oatmeal, then an important element in the Scottish worker's diet, had gone up from a shilling to one and fourpence a half stone, flour from a shilling to one and threepence or one and fivepence; sugar had increased from 2d to 3½d a pound, tea from 1s 2d to 1s 8d a pound; butter, cheese and meat had each gone up by 2d a pound. The price of fish had doubled. A hundredweight sack of coal cost 6d more than at the beginning of the war.

As the workers' resistance increased, the reactionaries set out to smear them. As early as April, Horatio Bottomley, editor of *John Bull*, made a speech in Glasgow denouncing strong drink and the drunkards whose drinking habits were alleged to be hindering the war effort. This speech was modelled on one made earlier in Parliament. Bottomley, later unmasked as a rogue, had a sliding scale of charges for his speeches. His highest charge was for a speech on imperialism. It is not known what he was paid for his speech downing the imperial gill and the imperial pint. In July, Basil Clark wrote an article in the *Daily Mail* attacking the high wages of Clyde workers. Apparently one of the signs of working-class debauchery was the sudden appearance of a rash of pianos in Paisley tenements. The improvident poor had become the improvident rich!

Speaking of the improvident poor, just after the events related above the story of one woman's suffering appeared in *The Bulletin*, a Glasgow pictorial newspaper. A woman about to give birth to her fifth child sought shelter for herself and her four children aged eleven, ten, six and four. Being herself poorly housed, the woman to whom she applied took her to the Parish Council chambers in John Street, on the north side of the river, in the city centre. On grounds that she was the responsibility of the old Govan Parish Council (Govan had been incorporated into Glasgow some three years previously), the official who interviewed her sent her to other offices in Carlton Place, south of the river. After some delay, she was told she must go back to John Street. She did so and was refused relief. Her next effort was to try to get a room in a tenement of sublet houses, but she was unsuccessful. By this time it was evening and the woman, desperate now, gave her purse to the children and told them to wait where they were, which was at the

foot of Clyde Street, near the river. Then a man waiting for the ferry
boat heard a splash and saw what he thought was a hand come up out
of the water. He alerted the ferry skipper, who rushed to the spot and
dragged the woman out with a boathook. She was carried ashore and
gave birth to her child on the ferry steps. The child was alive but died
later in hospital.

From the same paper we learn 'that in the course of her connection with the Work for Women Fund it has been borne in upon Queen
Mary strongly that dressmakers must live as well as other people and to
go to extremes in the matter of economy is to ruin. Consequently she
and Princess Mary dress as usual and show no signs of ostentatious
economy.' The sentiment is absolutely correct. There can be nothing
worse than ostentatious economy — except, perhaps, ostentatious
poverty.

Commenting on the general ferment of the time, the anonymous
writer of the *History of the Ministry of Munitions* says: 'It cannot be
doubted that this advance in rent together with the rise in the cost of
living were among the main causes of the very irritable temper which
the Munitions Acts inflamed into a fever'. The fever raged and the
Government, fearing the spread of its contagion rather than from any
regard for the people's well-being, decided that they must act. Certainly
it was not the fighting spirit of the Labour MPs that produced action.
Indeed, asked by the secretary of the Glasgow City Labour Party Housing Committee to move a resolution in Parliament asking the Government to suspend all increases in rent imposed since the start of the war,
Arthur Henderson replied that it would be advisable to prepare evidence before they could put down such a proposal. In fact, the secretary had already supplied this evidence in the form of increased rent
demand notices that had been gathered from all over the city and given
to George Barnes, MP for Blackfriars (now in Gorbals). Henderson had
admitted talking to Barnes. 'I think, after this experience, also the
events of more recent occurrence,' wrote the secretary in *Forward*,
'it will be clear to the minds of most of us that we need not depend on
the Labour Party in the House of Commons for support to any proposal that would betray a want of fidelity in His Majesty's Government'.

Reluctantly, after eight months of inaction, the Government
moved to grasp the nettle. They set up a Committee of Inquiry. (For
the benefit of younger readers it should be explained that committees
of inquiry are a means employed by governments to find out what
everybody else knows already.) The Committee of Inquiry consisted of
two men, Lord Hunter and Professor W R Scott, of Glasgow University.
Neither man was chosen for his known working-class sympathies. Lord
Hunter, formerly Liberal MP for Govan, had in the week prior to the
inquiry sittings in Glasgow, heard a case in Edinburgh in his capacity as
a Judge in the Scottish Court of Session. In that case he had decreed
that a bondholder who held a bond at 4 per cent on a property in

Airdrie, just outside Glasgow, should have his interest rate increased to 4½ per cent. The tenants of the property were the only source from which the bondholder's increase could come. Clearly, Lord Hunter was neutral, unbiased, and blind only in his left eye, like Justice herself. A number of people gave evidence to the Committee when it sat in Glasgow on 29 and 30 October. As John Wheatley, one of the witnesses, shrewdly pointed out, although many questions and answers turned on the question of the property bondholders, there was not one of them to give evidence. When his lordship was not asking questions that showed a lively concern for their well-being, he was asking about the cases of soldiers' dependants subjected to rent increases and threatened with eviction. Happily, at the beginning of October, Glasgow House Owners' Association had unanimously agreed that no advances should be intimated to tenants on active service with HM Forces. But the individual members continued their attempted extortions backed by threats of eviction.

The resolution passed at their meeting was simply an exercise in public relations for the benefit of Lord Hunter, Lloyd George and Asquith. Yet in the week following their pious resolution, in spite of a plea from McKinnon Wood, Secretary for Scotland, to 'hold their hand' pending the outcome of the inquiry, the factors issued notices of rent increases to thousands of tenants,applying rent increases of £1 to £3 a year, reinforcing their demand with a statement that unless the tenant renewed his let of his house at the increased rent, he and his family would be ejected on 28 November. The notice was fraudulent; before a tenant could be evicted he had to be taken to court under the Court Powers Emergency Act, 1914, where he could still plead against ejectment. The army of rent strikers swelled to 15,000 in Glasgow alone.

Wednesday, 17 November, must rank as one of the high points in British working-class history, standing with such events as the Jolly George incident, the General Strike, and the fight for the release of the Pentonville Five. On that day, 18 Glasgow tenants (15 of them munition workers) appeared to answer summonses taken out by their factor, one Nicholson, to show cause why they should not be evicted for refusal to pay increased rent. Thousands left their work that day, and several separate demonstrations converged on the city centre and the Small Debt Court. *Forward* estimated the crowd at 10,000, but peering through the miles and the miasma of political prejudice the *Manchester Guardian* counted only 4000. Perhaps it would be fair to say that gathered round the court that day was a crowd no bigger than a man's fist — a clenched fist. On their way from Govan one contingent marched to the school where John Maclean, already under notice of dismissal from Govan School Board, was teaching. He was taken out and carried shoulder high through the streets to the court, where he addressed the huge crowd from an improvised platform of newsagents' billboards held on comradely shoulders. The meeting resolved that unless the

Government acted to reduce rents to pre-war levels a general strike on the Clyde would follow.

Inside, the court was packed; only the Sheriff was absent. Willie Gallacher thought it probable that Sheriff Lee was on the telephone to the Government, seeking advice how to deal with the situation. This seems quite credible because, according to the statement by the factor's lawyer later that day, Lloyd George, Minister of Munitions, had on the previous day requested that the cases either be dropped or be continued later to allow the promised legislation to come into force. Another clue is that the court proceedings were timed to start at 10 am but Sheriff Lee did not appear in his court until after noon, and then only in response to loud cheering from the crowd, when Councillor Izett demanded to know who was responsible for the conduct of the court and, in the name of the workers there present, protested against the law's delays. The Sheriff appeared, rebuked all present and threatened to have the court cleared should there be any repetition of the disturbance.

On the Sheriff taking his seat, a rent strike leader, identified as Malcolm Nimmo in Tom Bell's *John Maclean — Fighter for Freedom*, asked him to meet a deputation and hear a statement which might have the effect of avoiding further trouble. The Sheriff replied that his function was a legal one and that he had no authority to mix himself up with political questions. These were exceptional times, however, and if it would effect the desired purpose he was prepared to take the risk of receiving a deputation.

A *Forward* representative accompanied the deputation to the Sheriff's private chambers. Perhaps alerted by 'the Chiel takin' notes', Sheriff Lee at the close of the interview suggested that in the special circumstances it might be better if it were regarded as more of a private meeting. So the *Forward* report carries only 'such parts of the interview as will give the workers on the Clyde an indication that the deputation accurately represented the views it was sent to represent.'

The first spokesman for the deputation was from Dalmuir Shipyard where, he said, 8000 men were prevailed upon to stay at work and send a deputation. He added: 'The country cannot do without these 8000 workers, but the country can do without the factors.' He stated that the factors ought to be charged under the Defence of the Realm Act. (Here spoke the voice of prophesy.) DORA was never used against rack-renters, but within a month or so of these events it was used by the Home Office to suppress *Forward* and have its offices occupied by the police. The paper's offence lay in telling the truth and insisting on its duty to inform. Lloyd George came to Glasgow to address the Clyde shop stewards. Reporters were not allowed into his meeting and the press was expected to print the official hand-out, thus giving the impression that 3000 shop stewards had had an improving afternoon, George the Father patiently explaining the great issues of state to the lower orders. Alas! one of their number took a shorthand note of the

Lloyd George debacle. *Forward* faithfully printed the man's report in full, beginning: 'Last Tuesday Mr Lloyd George, the best paid munitions worker in Britain, came to Glasgow in search of adventure. He got it.'

DORA was also used to put John Maclean in prison for three years on the conscription issue, then Gallacher and Maxton got one year each. Kirkwood and others were officially banished to Edinburgh, to be confined within a five-mile radius of that city under the step-fatherly eye of the Chief Constable, Colonel Levita. Kirkwood said they were 'legal revolutionaries'.

Another member of the deputation from Govan assured Sheriff Lee that theirs was not a spasmodic movement. The men considered the rent increases to be robbery. The Sheriff then delivered himself of one of the classic capitalist presentations of the law as impartial even-handed justice, fearing none and favouring none; a corpus of moral guidelines reinforced by sanctions; neither depending upon nor draw-ing upon class concepts of rent, interest and profit. He said he could only decide the case on strictly legal principles. His decision might be one that would meet with his sympathy or it might be quite contrary to all his sympathies. He had got to administer the law as he found it. What weighed with him in receiving that deputation at all was that they were living in exceptional times and under exceptional laws. With regard to many things our new laws — temporary laws — were fairly up-to-date and fairly defined, but with regard to some things discussion was just taking place, and the question of rents was one of these. The question they had got to consider was the advisability of forcing a deci-sion on these cases according to the law as it existed that day [the land-lord's law of eviction. *Ed*], when there might be new laws altogether in a week or two. The question they had got to consider was the advis-ability of forcing a decision. He would have thought it was better to wait to see whether there would be any legislation, and, with that in view, to ask for a continuation of these cases. It was said the temper of the strikers would not stand that. But why not? The tenants, as the factors, must recognise that when the law was fixed one way or the other, both sides would eventually have to obey. The country was embroiled in a great war, and the smallest cessation of work appreciably affected the progress of the war. He had no doubt they would do all they could to prevent the matter leading to trade disputes, which might cause inestimable harm. He again asked the deputation if it was not possible to wait for a week or two.

One of the deputation pointed out that workmen were prevented from leaving their particular work to go and better their positions; but the factor, who was under no Munitions Act, came along and raised the rents of those workmen. It was no use the deputation going back to the men with the suggestion to continue cases.

The Sheriff said he could not go into these political questions. He was trying to see whether by continuation he could put off a decision that might give offence and trouble outside. There might be new laws by another week, and he would have thought that if it were possible it would be better not to force a decision, but that was all he could do for them.

A worker said: 'We have left our work, and are determined not to go back unless you give a decision in favour of the tenant. It might look like coercion, and we are sorry, but we are anxious to avoid serious trouble. If you decide in favour of the tenants, it will be an indication to the Government to move in our favour.'

The Sheriff: 'Alas! alas! it is not my decision which will be an indication to the Government; it will be that horrible thought of industrial strife bringing untold misery into our midst.'

Shortly after these exchanges, the Sheriff returned to his court, where, after rebuking the house factor's lawyer for what he clearly regarded as a trespass on his authority, the Sheriff persuaded the factor not to seek a continuation of the case for another three weeks (the plan clearly proposed to the factor by the Ministry of Munitions, but which the Sheriff thought to be slighting and offensive to him and to his court for the manner in which it was settled, but rather to agree to drop the cases completely.

For the Government it was as well that Sheriff Lee's ideas prevailed that day. Had the cases been continued for three weeks, the fat would have been in the fire. Although the Increase of Rent and Mortgage Interest (War Restrictions) Bill was hurriedly introduced into Parliament on 25 November, it was not given the Royal Assent until 23 December. By his manoeuvres Sheriff Lee had saved himself in a Glasgow courtroom that day. His actions also prevented one of the greatest assaults on the system of Rent, Interest and Profit. R.I.P.

The army of rent strikers in Glasgow alone now stood at an estimated 25,000 and other towns and districts were also playing their part (a list of known places appears below) when the Government introduced its Rent and Mortgage (War Restrictions) Bill into the House of Commons on 25 November, 1915. The Minister responsible delivered himself of the thought that the war had brought cottage and castle closer together. Certainly the landlords and the house factors had done their level best to narrow the rent gap between the two types of property. The Liberals had been whipped into line, but their sorrow at the prospect of having to retreat from the principles enshrined in the philosophy of the market economy is patent for all to see in the pages of *Hansard*. The Government put up a feeble rearguard action, seeking to limit the action of the Bill to munition areas of not less than 100,000 population, but a number of MPs, reading the situation in their own constituencies, quickly put paid to that endeavour. The Government backed off in confusion. One MP described the measures as 'an unjust and necessary Bill', he thought it would not have been necessary had the Government acted six months sooner. Sir John Rolleston was impenitent. He said: 'I can only submit that the saving or thrifty man or woman who has taken the increased rent has been right to do so. It would have been wrong not to do so; to leave that money in the pocket of the well-to-do and the well-paid working man to spend on his numerous, and in many cases unwholesome pleasures.'

The good Sir John's words must have found an echo in the private thoughts of every pimp and pick-pocket and property owner in the land. What was being done in passing that measure confirmed Sir Frederick Banbury, a Tory, in his view that the Socialistic tendencies of George Barnes, Labour MP for Blackfriars (Glasgow), if pursued, would ruin the country in a very short time. Cowardly Sir Frederick to take advantage of Parliamentary immunity to libel Barnes as a socialist!

What of the Labour MPs? What did they do in the Great Rent War? Nothing of value that can be traced in the pages of *Hansard* or anywhere else. Barnes, representing the most congested slum in Britain, said little, and did not once refer to an important demand of the rent strikers and those who fought by their side: a return to the pre-war rent. Nor did any other Labour man raise this point at any time during the passage of the Bill. Very few of them spoke at all, and those who did, including Will Thorne, spoke like beggars.

The Bill received the Royal Assent on 23 December. Working-class people throughout the land had their rents frozen at the 3 August 1914 level. Key money and other premiums were forbidden and other important protections gained. Even lower middle class people got some relief thanks to the great rent struggle. Interest on mortgages was also limited to the levels in operation at the beginning of the war. Predictably the Bill contained provisions for the removal of control. But new struggles broke out and the control was not removed.

That was the way we lived then. The Housing Acts at that time were demolition oriented and the result was the destruction of insanitary areas, a synonym for the slums, and this they achieved by overcrowding. No houses were built with public money for the working class in the nineteenth century. So for much of this century, the working class remained effectively packed and boxed, and more horribly corralled than ever in old subdivided properties and the back-land stacked blocks standing on what once had been the greens. Slums were still profitable, the demolition sites clear and free for future gains.

In a survey for the Glasgow city authorities in 1965, *A Profile of Glasgow Housing*, the author, J B Cullingworth, revealed that the housing stock had scarcely improved; 85 per cent of all dwellings were flats and only 12 per cent houses. One third of all these dwellings contained only one or two rooms and 93 per cent lacked an internal water closet, 90 per cent had no bath; 11,000 dwellings were totally unfit, 75,000 were sub-standard and not fit for improvement at reasonable cost, 49,000 sub-standard but susceptible to improvement at reasonable cost.

Enid Gauldie, in her essay, *The Middle Class and Working Class*

Housing in the Nineteenth Century, draws the conclusion that 'in most towns speculative building of houses satisfied the demand, which because of the poverty of those in most need was low, but it did not attempt to fill the need. The confusion between need and demand had delayed the solution of the housing problem from the beginning. Those in need created no demand....' Sir Patrick Geddes writes in *Cities in Evolution:* 'The weakness and confusion of the middle-class ideas left the way open to those with clear direction, no confusion about their motives, no doubt about the right way to behave. Those who speculated in land, those who drew rents from overcrowded insanitary property, those who put up jerry-built rows could benefit from reformers' confusion.'

There was, and remains to this day, no confusion in the minds of those who floated the capital and those who built the new housing. The new housing was built for those who had the money to pay for it. It was built in new areas away from the labouring mass. Housing had always reflected class difference and does so now in the appalling tower block developments thrown up in recent years. The new system clearly defined class division. Even in death the classes were now clearly distinguished. The death rate in the ghettoes of the poor was twice, often three times, higher than that in the new suburbs. The speculative use of land and the role of the usurer imposed a pattern on all subsequent new housing provision. Some thought has been given to planning, none to the stifling effect of interest burdens. But the first task is to plan the society in which we live. We must plan for use, not for profit. The rule applies to housing as much as to any other commodity.

Footnote: In our researches for this article we have established that rent strikes took place in the following places in 1915:
Scotland – Glasgow: Govan, Partick, Parkhead, Pollockshaws, Pollock, Cowcaddens, Kelvingrove, Ibrox, Govanhill, St Rollox, Townhead, Springburn, Maryhill, Fairfield, Blackfriars (Gorbals) and Woodside.
Aberdeen, Dundee, Greenock, Clydebank, Cambuslang, Hamilton, Annan Gretna, West Calder and in Fife and Mid Lanark.
Wales – Cardiff and Merthyr Tydfil .
England – London: East Ham, Canning Town, Poplar, Plaistow, Plumstead, Ilford, Woolwich, Stoke Newington, Brixton, Acton, Forest Gate, Barrow, Birkenhead, Newcastle, Manchester, Bury St Edmunds, Liverpool, Birtley, Halifax, Market Harborough, Letchworth, Salford, Coventry and Leicester.
If you know of other places please write to the authors care of BOOKMARKS.

3 The forty hours strike
John Leopold

The forty hours strike in Scotland in January and February 1919 was an important testing ground for the development of the revolutionary movement in Britain. As the demand for the 35-hour week is raised today to absorb the unemployed, the story of the 40 hours' strike has much to teach us.

The problem of what to do about the large numbers of soldiers who would be returning to civilian life after the war had been worrying the Labour Movement for some time. As early as April 1918, the Scottish Trades Union Congress had passed a motion for a 30-hour week to absorb the unemployed. By the end of 1918, there were 30,000 unemployed in Glasgow alone, and the bulk of the demobilisation had not yet begun.

Glasgow was hit sooner than most towns with unemployment, as ship-building, engineering, and munition work geared to the war effort were run down. During the war, unemployment in ship-building was 0.15 per cent. But on 3 January 1919 it was 2.1 per cent, by February 4.9 per cent. In engineering it rose from a wartime average of 0.5 per cent to 8 per cent in January, and 11 per cent by February.

Soldiers, promised a land fit for heroes, returned to the dole queue. Trade unionists in ship-building and engineering, despite the struggles of 1915 and 1916, had seen conditions eroded to aid the war effort. Now that the war was over, Labour was demanding a better deal.

However, after the coupon election of December 1918, which returned a landslide majority for the coalition national government, there seemed little chance of gains coming through Parliament. Clydeside returned only one Labour MP, Neil McLean for Govan. Even John Maclean, recently appointed Soviet ambassador in Britain, failed to defeat a pro-coalition Labour candidate in the Gorbals, such was the hysteria for the coalition government. The working class had to look to themselves for any improvements in their conditions.

The engineering workers' union, the Amalgamated Society of Engineers, had agreed with the engineering employers for a 47-hour week to start at the beginning of January 1919. In a ballot of members this was accepted 36,000 votes to 28,000. A close decision, but one which was to cause problems for the militant engineers who wanted hours reduced more.

However, support for 47 hours was by no means universal, even among official bodies. In August 1918, the Scottish advisory committee of the Labour Party, the Parliamentary Committee of the STUC, and the Glasgow Trades Council had jointly approached the government on getting a 40-hour week.

Many rank and file workers were more determined. Few Glasgow branches of the ASE supported the 47 hours. Many were for 30. The question of hours had to be linked with that of overtime. The Glasgow 7 branch demanded that the District Committee (which was for 30 hours) call an overtime ban: 'as in some establishments men are being paid off, whilst others in the same shop are working overtime.'

The link between unemployment and the weakening of trade union organisation was made clear in a later strike bulletin: 'When we are all employed in useful labour at Union rates we cannot be used to reduce wages....when there is unemployment we lose control and the profiteers rob us as they please.'

The normal working week up to 1919 was 54 hours, 6 am - 5.30 pm Monday to Friday and 6 am to 12.30 pm on Saturdays. One worker, Tom Bell, at the time President of the Scottish Iron-Moulders, describes what it was like to work those hours:

'I had to be up at 4.45 every morning to walk a mile for a train to Shettleston in time for a 6 o'clock start. We stopped at 5.30 pm and if it was necessary to work overtime it was about 9 pm before I got home.'

In the euphoria after the war, and with hopes high for a general improvement in conditions, the solution of a 47-hour week did not seem a good enough improvement on the old system. The vote in the ASE had been carried narrowly, largely because it had been posed in terms of 47 or 54 hours. No other number was on the ballot paper. The rest of the unions in the Confederation of Shipbuilding and Engineering Workers who voted accepted 47 hours with the exception of the Boiler-makers and the Shipwrights. Support for a shorter working week increased when the 47 hours was implemented in January 1919, when it became clear that breakfast had to be taken before arriving at work at 7.30 am and that there would be no meal break at 9 am. Thus people had to get up at much the same time as before and they didn't finish any earlier. Further, although the decrease to 47 hours was without loss of pay on time rates, it was also to be without loss of production. In short, they were being sold a productivity deal.

In a number of workplaces on Clydeside, such as Dumbarton Dock-yard, there was no restart on the first day after the holiday. Thus the new 47-hour week negotiated by the ASE executive got off to a rough start.

However, moves were afoot on Clydeside to achieve a much more fundamental change in hours, wages, and conditions. On Sunday 5 January a conference of Clydeside shop stewards rejected the 47-hour week as a means of increasing productivity and hence unemployment. They elected a Ways and Means Committee of eight to bring all the shop stewards in the area together with a mandate from their respective workshops, in the hope of taking united action on a given date.

Factory gate meetings were organised and shop floor votes taken. A further conference was held in Glasgow on 16 January with delegates from all over Scotland. Well over half the workshops where a vote had been taken were for a week of 30 hours. Only one was for 47 hours. The rest were for 40 hours.

At this conference the rank and file of the shop stewards movement came together with levels of the trade union bureaucracy — the Parliamentary Committee of the STUC; the Executive of the Glasgow Trades Council, and the Joint District Committees of the Shipbuilding and Engineering trades. At this conference there were disagreements between the official movement, who were all for 40 hours and who in the case of the STUC wanted the strike delayed for two weeks, and the shop stewards' movement who had support for 30 hours. The strike was set for 27 January with a sub-committee of the elected joint committee left to decide the actual demand.

The lack of total agreement and clarity of purpose between the shop stewards' movement and the local bureaucracy was made much worse by the attitude of the executives of most of the unions involved. The divisions were to give the employers and the government the opportunity to divide and rule. While a number of local trade union officials like Harry Hopkins, Glasgow District Secretary of the ASE, and Tom Bell, President of the Scottish Ironmoulders, backed the strike, most national executives were firmly against it. Only the moulders, the Electrical Trade Union and one or two smaller societies backed it and authorised strike pay.

The unofficial nature of the strike incurred the combined wrath of the ASE executive, the TUC, the Engineering Employers, the Press and the Government. The existence of the 47 hours agreement between the employers and the ASE executive was used to drive a wedge between the mass of the strikers and the shop stewards.

A statement from the engineering employers before the strike made the position clear:

'Under existing arrangements all difficulties must be referred for discussion to the Joint Committees of Employers and Workpeople set up for the pupose. But obviously such a discussion cannot take place unless the workpeople are prepared to let their representatives participate unhindered by complications arising from stoppages of work.'

Or, in other words, joint negotiating committees were there to supercede strikes and union executives were to make sure no unofficial strikes took place.

The attempts to prevent the strike failed. The first day, 27 January, saw an estimated 40,000 out. That figure was to grow to more than 100,000 on the Clyde plus some 14,000 on the Forth by the end of the week.

The strike was by no means confined to Glasgow. Engineering and ship-building workers on both sides of the Clyde, in Dumbarton and in Paisley were out on the Monday. 8,000 struck in the Leith shipyards, as did large numbers of engineering and printing workers in Edinburgh. The naval dockyards in Rosyth were severely affected, and 1000 workers were out in Grangemouth. On 28 January a delegate conference of strikers was held in Glasgow. Delegates attended from as far away as Dumfries, Dundee, and Alloa, as did delegates from Belfast, Grimsby, and Rugby.

In West Fife, the miners in Cowdenbeath had struck on 23 January for the re-establishment of demobilised tradesmen. They were supported by Bowhill, Lochgelly, and Glencraig pits. Over the weekend, the miners' rank and file organisation, the Fife Miners Reform Committee, campaigned in the militant areas and the demand for a six hour, five day week was adopted.

On 30 January a 10,000 strong demonstration of miners marched from the West Fife coalfield to Dunfermline to gain official support for the strike. But the local officials campaigned against the strike in East Fife and in a ballot of all Fife miners there was a small majority for a return to work.

The situation in the Lanarkshire coalfield was similar. On 27 January many Lanarkshire miners ignored an appeal from the Scottish Executive of their union to stay at work. As the local paper reported: 'This delaration had little or no effect on the situation.' The strike spread on the Tuesday, and again on the Wednesday, when mass pickets brought out pits in the Hamilton area and extended the strike to Holytown.

On the Wednesday afternoon, 1500 strikers, including those from as far away as Shotts, held a mass meeting in Hamilton Public Park. Again union officials urged them to return until national negotiations were complete. Instead they agreed to stay out and to send a delegation to the Executive Committee of the Lanarkshire miners to urge a ballot on the strike question.

On the Wednesday evening, there was a mass demonstration of miners outside the Union HQ in Hamilton. The offices were occupied; red banners flown from the balcony; and the crowd sang the Red Flag while the delegates from the Lanarkshire Reform Committee met the executive.

The executive were forced to call an all-Lanarkshire strike on the Thursday when further demonstrations 15,000 strong took place in Hamilton. Another one-day stoppage was called for the Friday.

To escape the pressure of the rank and file, the Lanarkshire executive were forced to meet in Edinburgh on the Saturday, when they recommended a return to work. Only a few pits were still out on the Monday and by the Tuesday it was only Shettleston and Tolcross who held out.

The Hamilton local paper condemned the mass picketing which the miners had adopted as a tactic in the dispute. Its success forced the mine managers to call for tighter laws on picketing. These same tactics were adopted in other areas with remarkable success.

The mass picket was first seen on the Monday. After deciding to strike, 2000 workers at the Albion Motor plant marched en masse to Barr and Stroud and pulled them out. At Dalmuir, Beardmore's was closed as a result of a mass picket. John Brown's in Clydebank was the next target on the Tuesday. From the first day of the strike, workers in Dumbarton held mass meetings which decided which factories to picket. The organised unemployed also made their point by picketing factories still working, urging the men to come out.

On the Tuesday in Dumbarton, 5000 marched through the town. As the local paper remarked somewhat apprehensively: 'no strike demonstration like it was ever seen in Dumbarton before.' The 5000 formed a mass picket at Dennystoun Forge and at Babcock and Wilcox's tube works, closing both. By the Wednesday night, the whole area was at a standstill.

On the Thursday, the strikers marched from Dumbarton up the Vale of Leven, blocking the tramway en route, to the munition works at Alexandria which were still working. They, too, joined the strike. The Dumbarton strikers were even considering ways of bringing out the office workers in the area.

The picture south of the Clyde was no different. In Paisley, mass meetings of strikers were held each morning at the cross. After hearing reports on the strike's progress, they decided where to picket that lunchtime. On the Wednesday, they marched down Love Street, 'which for a time presented a spectacle such as may be witnessed on a Saturday when a big football match is on at St Mirren's Park.' Love Street was not the target, but the works in Inchinnan Road.

It was in this way that the strength of mass action was revealed. Workers in Clydebank, Dumbarton, Hamilton, Glasgow, Paisley and elsewhere adopted the same tactics. The strikers were kept informed of the situation by the daily mass meetings and by the strike bulletin which was produced daily from the Wednesday. By these methods the press attacks on the strikers could be countered; and more importantly the strikers could be involved in strengthening their strike by their own actions.

One of the mass meetings in Glasgow made the position of the rank and file absolutely clear:

'This meeting pledges its support to the joint committee and urges it to prosecute the strike with the utmost vigour until the Government is forced to open up negotiations with the committee, and that when this is done the committee should submit the Government's proposals to the rank and file, with a view to a satisfactory settlement on the basis of the 40 hours week for all time, piece, and lieu workers, without any reduction of wages.'

In each district strike committees ran the strike and held mass meetings daily, as in Paisley and Dumbarton. Each committee had to send a delegate to the information bureau each day at 11 am to report news in their locality. Then they returned to their district by 2.30 pm to report to their strike committee and back to the bureau for 4 pm. Thus reliable lines of communication were kept intact and up-to-date information could be put in the daily strike bulletin.

The strike committees also took on a social function, organising concerts to keep the strikers entertained in the afternoons. Bands also played an important part in rallying the strikers in the demonstrations.

The war had seen an increase in the numbers of women working and, at its end, women were usually first down the road. By January 1919, it was reckoned that there were 22,195 unemployed women in Glasgow alone. The Scottish section of the Federation of Women Workers gave the strike full support. In Clydebank, a special meeting was held for the women of the town, which voted to support the strike. They did so actively — successfully picketing apprentices trying to attend a Loyalist meeting. Similar support came from women in Bridgeton, Partick, Govan, and Dumbarton. The *Paisley Express* noted the zeal with which the women participated: 'It was noted that the women were not silent onlookers but in some cases showed more zeal and demonstrated more in speech than the men.'

In most histories of the period it is the events in George Square, Glasgow, on Friday 31 January which gain most attention.

Following a demonstration to George Square on the Wednesday to demand that Lord Provost Stewart request the Government to intervene and concede the demands, the Lord Provost told them to come back at 12.30 on 31 January for the reply.

The Government was clearly trying to drive a wedge between the shop stewards' leaders and the union officials, and thus break the strike. Bonar Law, the Prime Minister, telegrammed the Lord Provost to say:

'the Government are unable to entertain requests for intervention made by local members of unions, whose representatives are acting for them in conference with the employers.

'Such action on the part of the Government could only undermine the authority of those who have been chosen by the men to
represent their interests, and would destroy that co-operation
between employers and employed on which the hopes of industrial peace depends.'

The Government, however, were quite prepared to intervene
against the local members of unions and did so in George Square on the
Friday, when some 30,000 strikers turned up to hear the Government's
reply.

The police, who had been present in force on the Wednesday, used
the excuse of the need to keep the tram lines running to attack a section of the crowd. How trams were to move through 30,000 people
remains an unsolved mystery.

Neutral observers were clear that the police started the fighting.
The *Daily News* reporter wrote on 3 February 1900: 'I have no hesi-
tation in saying that the baton charge made with the object of clearing
a way for a tram car was the beginning of the trouble.'

The crowd gave as good as they got in the fray that followed. One
section commandeered a lemonade lorry in North Frederick Street to
reply to the blows of the police batons. Willie Gallacher made his
famous attack on the Chief Constable, to be promptly struck down by
a police baton.

The crowd only dispersed when told by the leaders to go to Glasgow
Green. Their leaders, Gallacher, Shinwell and Kirkwood, were arrested.
Near Glasgow Green, the police attempted to stop the demonstration
but were forced to back down by the strikers who went on to the
Green to have their meeting.

By the next morning, Glasgow was an armed camp. Highland and
English troops were used lest the strikers tried to disaffect the local
troops at Maryhill barracks. As a recent historian has remarked: 'That
Glasgow could have been placed under armed occupation without prior
planning and consultation is inconceivable.'

The Government had issued its reply to the strikers. It did not end
the strike immediately but during the next week reports of places going
back to work began to trickle in. The mass picketing which had been so
successful in the first week did not take place that week, and attacks on
the strikers by the press and by the trade union officialdom increased.

The Parliamentary Committee of the TUC (the forerunner of the
General Council) sent out a manifesto to its affiliates, saying:

'The TUC Parliamentary Committee deem it necessary to circularise
the officials and members of the organisations concerned in order
that the hands of the responsible leaders of the Trade Union movement may be strengthened and the unions governed in an orderly
and regular manner.'

The daily strike bulletin was used to counter the bourgeois press,
selling up to 20,000 copies a day at 1d. In the second week, trams were

only allowed to run in Dumbarton if they carried the strike commit-tee's information sheets in their windows. A boycott of the *Daily Record* was ordered, yet false reports about the end of the strike appeared which helped sow confusion in the ranks.

As the strike wore on to its second week only the ironmoulders were receiving strike pay. The shortage of money, combined with attacks on the shop stewards in contrast to the responsible trade union leaders, and the presence of the troops, obviously undermined the will of many of those involved.

The key lay in spreading the strike to other parts. Belfast had been out since 25 January for 44 hours. There the control of the city was almost totally in the hands of the strike committee. As Tom Bell later wrote: 'Permission, under stipulations to take ships out of dry dock, could only be obtained from the strike committee. To pass along Queens Road to the shipyards a permit was necessary.'

After Bloody Friday delegates were sent from Glasgow to English centres to try and spur on the threatened strikes there. Delegates from England had been present at a number of strike meetings on the Clyde. A South Wales Miners Federation delegate had spoken at a mass meet-ing of Denny's shipyard workers on 15 January.

The strike bulletins always contained details of the Belfast strike. It also reported international events like the strike of Bombay dock workers; the General Strike in Seattle, USA, for a shorter working week; and strikes in Japan. Throughout the second week of the bulletin, hopeful reports of the strike spreading to London, Sheffield, Tyneside, Barrow and Manchester appeared.

That action did not materialise. Although some shipyard workers on Tyneside, Birkenhead and Hull came out on unofficial strike, much depended on the engineers. In most areas, revolutionaries were not in control of district committees, as on the Clyde. The ASE executive did its utmost to hold back action, so much so that when London shop stewards voted for strike action police had to guard the ASE HQ in case there was a protest demonstration.

It was the electricians who officially backed the 40 hours' strike. But the Government intervened quickly, using the Defence of the Realm Act to keep the power stations open. Strikers were made liable to a six-month jail sentence or a £100 fine, or both.

Over the weekend of 8-9 February, the confusion sown by the ASE executive, which had suspended the entire Glasgow, Belfast, and London District Committees on 6 February, led to a number of ASE branches voting to return. The other areas were divided over support for 47, 44, or 40 hours. Although most wanted a reduction, the opposition of the executive undermined support for strike action to achieve the demands.

On the Clyde, the joint committee decided to suspend the strike and recommend a return to work until such time as a national campaign for 40 hours could be launched. The majority of the workers returned on the Wednesday, except the ironmoulders, whose official strike ended on the Thursday.

The trial of those arrested in George Square came in April. Eight of the accused, including the ASE Glasgow District Secretary, Harry Hopkins, were acquitted. Emmanuel Shinwell got six months for incitement to riot. Willie Gallacher and two others got three months.

Gallacher's reminiscences of the trial are both amusing and tragic. The police claimed that stones, chunks of iron and bottles had been thrown at them in front of the City Chambers before they made their baton charge. Despite this, the police could not explain why none of the many windows in front of the City Chambers, nor any of the four lamp-posts, each with a cluster of seven arc globes, were broken. The strikers must have had an extremely accurate aim. Photographs taken after the demo show the whole roadway in front of the City Chambers.... 'but not a sign, not the slightest vestige of a missile anywhere.'

The strike, then, was defeated despite the tremendous solidarity of those involved. Unemployment continued to rise, especially after the post-war boom collapsed in 1920. In Glasgow, unemployment rose to 16 per cent in 1920, and 25 per cent in 1923. The employers used the slump to win back many of the concessions made during the war, preparing the ground for the defeat of the General Strike.

While the 40 hours was not achieved in 1919, there was a general reduction in hours. The 47-hour week arrived in ship-building and engineering; farmworkers got a 50-hour week; most corporation workers got a 48-hour week; carters 48; builders 44 — all without loss of pay.

Clearly the ability of the employers to use the machinery of the state to protect their interest was a decisive factor in crushing the strike. Many of the leading employers were reported to be in the City Chambers before the police attack on the 31 January. The press, both local and national, consistently supported the employers and attempted to undermine the strike. Indeed on Monday 10 February the Glasgow evening paper reported that the strike was over, thus forcing the hand of the strike committee.

However, the collapse of the strike cannot be blamed on the employers alone. We also need to look at the enemy within. The final issue of the strike bulletin was clear as to where a lot of the blame lay:

> 'Don't forget the executives who failed us in the fight. These elected servants of ours who have become our bosses are not too favourable to the 40 hours movement. They are evidently afraid that it would reduce the bosses' profits, and that would never do! If we don't put our executives in order, we will get nowhere, as every time we make an improvement in our conditions they generally assist big business to keep us from winning.'

The ASE executive, in particular, did everything it could to undermine the strike — not making it official; suspending the Glasgow,

Belfast, and London District Committees, threatening to suspend other English District Committees who supported the action. Their position allowed the Government and the employers to refuse even to talk to the joint committee on the grounds that an agreement had been made with the ASE executive and they could not go back on it.

The contrast with the ironmoulders is most obvious. They supported the strike, made it official and paid strike pay. Indeed, they imposed fines on recalcitrant districts for not obeying the strike call. Their position did not come about by accident, but because Tom Bell, the president, and other members of the executive, were members of the Socialist Labour Party and had the support of the best organised, most militant factories.

There was a need to prepare the ground for the strike in other areas so that attempts by union executives to undermine the action could be defeated. A mechanism for doing this existed through the National Committee of Shop Stewards, but this was not done. Although delegates went out to other areas after Bloody Friday, the need was for a coherent rank and file movement based in the workplaces to co-ordinate and spread the demand for 40 hours. Without such an organisation, the officials could, and did, isolate and defeat the militant areas.

A similar problem applied to the relationship between unions. Rank and file militants had been in the vanguard of moves towards amalgamation before the war. The development of workshop organisation cut across craft boundaries in engineering and shipbuilding. Although in the best-organised workshops all trades came out, there were many reports of only partial success in gaining support for the strike as certain trades stayed in. A similar situation arose at the end of the strike, boilermakers and shipwrights holding out as their piece work based earnings would be adversely affected in the 47-hour week as it stood.

A particular problem was spreading the strike beyond the metal trades, where the workshop organisation was strongest. Although the Lanarkshire and Fife miners, through the pressure of their reform committees, came out during the first week of the strike, their executive persuaded them to go back until the negotiations with the employers were complete. They ended in deadlock and a ballot of the membership was overwhelmingly in favour of strike action for a six-hour, five-day week. But the strike was postponed with the setting up of the Sankey Commission, which gave the employers and the Government time to prepare their ground.

John Maclean wanted the 40 hours' strike postponed for a month so that the miners would join. But the action of the Fife and Lanarkshire miners showed that they were ready to join and efforts should have been made to spread the strike to other areas then. Maclean himself was in England during most of the strike and played no part in it. Although the miners' executive gave a lead a few weeks later, by then it was too late and the miners were on their own.

If the development of a national rank and file movement capable of taking control of the movement when the officials failed was lacking, so too was the existence of a revolutionary organisation capable of developing the strike into a challenge for power.

Many members of the strike committee were members of the British Socialist Party or the Socialist Labour Party, and the strike bulletin was printed on the SLP press. J T Murphy, a leading member of the SLP, wrote in their weekly paper *The Socialist* on 6 February: 'The conditions at present, in this revolutionary period, are such that we, with a little audacity, can provoke a crisis if we have but the courage.'

The courage may well have been there, but the organisational depth and penetration into the organised working class was lacking. SLP militants in other areas had not been able to develop a rank and file movement in industry to help spread the strikes. Their paper had only just turned weekly but its orientation and style was still that of a magazine rather than an agitational paper.

The paper was not used during the strike to agitate for spreading and developing the action. And the SLP had not yet assimilated the organisational and political lessons of the October Revolution. In short, they were not yet a revolutionary party capable of leading the working class to power.

Yet the 40 hours strike was a remarkable period in working-class history, one which has been neglected and ignored by most accounts of the period. The self-organisation of the strike meetings, social activities and mass pickets of the first week still stands as a lesson to socialists and militants today. So, too, does the attitude and actions of the union officials and the need to build an independent movement to supercede them when they betray their members.

The Scottish workers on the Clyde did not see themselves as separate from the English or indeed the world working class. They were the vanguard of the struggle for all workers. In reporting the Bombay dockworkers' strike, the *Strike Bulletin* proudly proclaimed: 'A victory in Scotland will help our comrades in India, who are with us in heart and soul.' They did not want nor seek the barrier of nationalism; they had barriers enough with the employers, the press, the state, and their own officials.

4 The present is history
Dave Sherry

'A time of sowing, and a time of reaping
And a time to reward the robbers.'

Mary MacDonald of Skeabost and Glasgow, poet of the clearances and of a wounded and exploited people, wrote those words nigh on a century ago. Since then, thousands of people have yearned, worked and agitated for that time to come. It might just be that the time to reward the robbers is, today, closer than any of us think.

There is a restless searching going on. Old horizons and taken-for-granted political structures are being called into question. There is massive inflation, savage cuts in public spending and tough wage controls at a time when prices are rocketing and fortunes being made. There is considerable appetite for real, not imaginary social change. It is this that has prompted the rapid growth of the SNP.

What you have in mind by way of change depends very much upon who you are and what class you come from. For the professional politicians and middle-class aspirants who lead the SNP at virtually every level, the aim is to substitute a gilded capitalist Scotland for the once treasured but now irrevocably decayed British version.

But among ordinary working-class people, who for so long trusted their fate to Labour, the appetite is whetted by altogether different prospects. There is a deep desire for real power and control over the blind economic and political processes that cripple and stunt our lives. There is a real concern to see an end to the grim poverty and endless unemployment which disfigures this society. The circumstances are remarkable, taken one by one. In combination they are little short of devastating, an indication not that society as we know it *might* approach a whole series of crossroads, but that it *is* approaching them. It is therefore a time of unparalleled opportunity for the socialist movement, provided always that people stick by what they believe in and try to build.

Unfortunately the growth of the SNP is so considerable that a number of socialists are simply looking for shelter. Some, like Eric Heffer, search for it in the sanctity of the British state. Others, like the writer and poet Alan Bold, travel in the opposite direction.

Bold, a former left-wing — even revolutionary — socialist, is now so drunk with the wine of independence that he really does seem to believe that just by changing the Royal High School in Edinburgh into a sovereign assembly, ordinary people's lives will be significantly transformed.

And yet, despite his intoxication, this recently-repented editor of the *Penguin Book of Socialist Verse* still entertains the odd doubt or reservation. In a recent issue of a magazine called *Scotia Review*, he writes: 'Independence for Scotland is coming.... But independence will have to be in the interests of the national community — or we in Scotland will be ruled by little Englanders with a difference.

'There could be businessmen who want to monopolise the wealth of the newly recognised nation; there could be careerist politicians who see more chance of making high office in a country of 5 million people than in a country of 45 million people.'

There could be businessmen who want to monopolise wealth. There could be ! Brother Bold, we've got news for you. There are droves of them, some with familiar names like Fraser or Younger or Noble. Others, less well-known, are the dedicated servants of profit hungry multinationals, organisations which have never anywhere found a shortage of careerist politicians ready to do their bidding.

The SNP leaders are only too clear in their own minds just who is to benefit from the Scotland they have in mind. That's why they strain every muscle to keep their supporters locked in the vault of orthodox electoral politics. And that's why their policies are in no way even mildly radical.

As Gordon Brown rightly puts it in his introduction to *The Red Paper on Scotland:* 'The SNP's "new politics" which "reject class warfare" presumes the familiar priorities of wealth and power over people. Their incoherence over the impact of multinationals on the Scottish economy, their rejection of the public ownership of land, oil and basic industries, and their corresponding faith in incentives and local entrepreneurship is a familiar blend of the old well-worn formulas, which assumes the subservience of Scottish workers to private international controls.'

Gordon Brown and his fellow contributors to *The Red Paper* haven't in the main jumped on the nationalist bandwagon. But they peddle another set of comfortable illusions. For in so far as *The Red Paper on Scotland* has an ounce of strategy, this urges us to rely on the very professional politicians and trade union bureaucrats whose abject failure is one of the main motors for the growth of the SNP.

Gordon Brown and Co all believe that somewhere along the line
there is a wonder drug for an incapacitated Labour Party. If the right
resolution is carried, the leopard (now in its dotage) will change its
spots. Gordon Brown does, of course, refer to the appalling poverty
that is the inevitable accompaniment of capitalism's princely incomes
for the few. And he is sincerely shocked and horrified by the system.
But what does he propose we do about it? Why, we're to have 'a social
audit of people's needs'. That is, instead of actually doing anything
about poverty, we're to grab hold of a ruler and go out and measure it
once again.

In between our sorties, to measure a problem whose dimensions
are only too apparent to the people who're on the receiving end, we're
once again to put our faith, our touching faith, in resolutions from the
TUC or the STUC. If read repeatedly even the most abject compromise
can start to sound vaguely left-wing, another notch in the record of 'left
advance' which enables the faithful to pretend that while the crab has
has actually moved sideways once again, it has at least contrived the
appearance of moving forward.

So *The Red Paper*, full of useful facts and information, is of little
or no value when it comes to the 64,000 dollar question: What can
ordinary people do to further the cause of socialism?

Alan Bold and others like him say that we should sit back and hope
that independence will be 'in the interests of the national community',
whatever that may be. Gordon Brown and Co get the warm glow inside
through another method of doing nothing. They live in hope that another alleged left-winger will scale the heights of the STUC General
Council or the Labour Party executive. A left-dominated assembly, plus
a left-dominated General Council, is their recipe for real social change.

The first thing we can all do is stick this particular set of illusions
in the left luggage and throw away the ticket. One piece of agitation for
the cause among your fellow workers, the rank and file in the factories
and on the housing estates, is worth any amount of so-called left advance
on the General Council. For ordinary working men and women do have
the power and potential to change society. The TUC General Council, by
contrast, have the power to numb the mind, and a not inconsiderable
interest in persistently doing so.

We can make a good start in the struggle to build and project a
genuine socialist alternative simply by refusing any longer to kid people
that anything apart from their own energies and organisation will ever
change their lives in any fundamental way.

The case for this kind of uncompromising socialist alternative has
been argued clearly and with considerable passion in the recent Socialist
Workers Party publication *Why you should be a socialist*. A short
quotation from that pamphlet which has sold in some thousands of
copies to workers throughout Scotland, is not out of place:

'....the central argument for a strong socialist party is founded in the strength and co-ordination of capitalism....Capitalists quarrel from time to time. They argue about tactics and squabble over their ill-gotten gains. But in the face of workers' resistance they join ranks and co-ordinate their forces. If the workers are to break that machine, they too need centralised and disciplined organisation. They too need to be able to move quickly and link up their power. Once co-ordinated, their power is far stronger than that of the capitalists, but unless it is co-ordinated, the capitalists can divide and rule....'

Such centralised and disciplined organisation will be just as essential whether or not independence comes to Scotland. For the same multinationals will dominate the economy. Their property 'rights' will be protected by the same police force. There may well be a Scottish Army nominally separate from an English one. But that army will be a part of some military alliance which binds together army bosses from many, many countries with a view to deploying military force in a concerted fashion against any radical developments anywhere.

In outlining the beginnings of a socialist strategy, *Why you should be a socialist* continues:

'The International Socialists (now the Socialist Workers Party) started in the early 1960s as a very small "fringe group". We were sustained by a number of ideas which marked us off from other socialists. We argued that the apparently benign and stable capitalism of that time would not last, that it was propped up by arms spending which carried in itself the seeds of contradiction and crisis; and that Labour government would be impotent to resist the demands of capitalism as it slumped into that crisis.

'We argued for a new rank and file socialist party. But above all we argued that such a party could not be built separately from the lives and conditions of the working people. It had to be a party *of* the working people which lived and breathed real lives and real aspirations. It was impossible to think straight without involving ourselves and acting with workers who were not yet convinced, without talking and writing in a language which people understood.'

Now these are first principles rather than strategy. But these principles inform and determine the strategy. Throughout, the emphasis is on self-activity, on do-it-yourself politics, on organisation from the bottom up. And whether Scotland becomes independent or not, the need for that emphasis will remain. For no parliament whatever its name or location can yield really decisive social change.

Shorn of this self-activity, socialism is neither possible nor meaningful. Only mass action can promote change and only mass action can sustain, consolidate and spread it to other countries. So if the goal is self-activity, so, too, is the means. It is the job of any socialist worthy of the name to promote that capacity for self-activity and self-emancipation, to find ways to scale it down from a long-term concern to a workaday reality.

This means involving oneself in the here and now. It means focusing attention and concern on the existing struggles of working people. It means searching for ways to help sharpen and strengthen those struggles and help speed victory.

It means trying to give organisational form to the desire for militant action and real social change inside the existing organisations of the working class. It means trying to build up rank and file organisation in order to stiffen resistance to unemployment, the cuts and wage controls. It means producing rank and file bulletins and newpapers to further the cause of unity in action. It means that knowledge got in books must be applied in propaganda work, doing street meetings, writing, producing and distributing socialist propaganda, in socialist discussion groups and, where possible, building party branches at work.

It means devising a variety of ways of reaching a much wider audience and doing everything in your power to project the full-blooded socialist alternative.

In the great explosion of struggle set out earlier in this book, the possibilities and the problems are clear for all to see. Who can deny that the working class has the capacity to run society after reading only a little of its history, for once honestly presented? But this being said, it is also pretty clear that the working class needs decisive leadership from within its ranks to win through. If decisive leadership is not forthcoming then indecisive leadership will be. And so, instead of spreading a struggle, the indecisive once again will go begging the Lord Provost or some other important person for a settlement to get themselves off the hook.

The history of the class struggle is also the history of agitation and organisation. From the period described earlier in this book emerged the small but nevertheless influential Communist Party. In Scotland today that party still has considerable influence. Its leaders get a good deal of their credibility from the heritage of rank and file struggle for socialism. But today their policies are in direct contradiction to that heritage. Like Gordon Brown, they have endless illusions about 'left advance' via the STUC General Council. Like him they put their faith in parliament and a sovereign assembly, rather than in the self-organisation and self-activity of the working class.

In earlier times, the Communist Party was not wholly preoccupied with winning friends and influence in high places. It was for the rank and file fight for socialism. But today the Communist Party is completely oriented on the parliamentary road to nowhere and to its marriage partner, the pursuit of careers and bureaucratic position in the trade union movement.

The Communist Party has a considerable working-class base. But that base is rarely mobilised in anything approximating a full sense. And even then, the desire for parliamentary friends and union influence straitjackets and blocks the potential unleashed.

The great struggle at UCS is a case in point. This was indeed a struggle of historic proportions which prompted quite new developments throughout the working class of Scotland, Wales and England. But if any parliamentary oriented political party in Scotland can be said to have benefited from the struggle, then surely it must have been the SNP. For them, the UCS atmosphere was very much part of the lift-off. Why was this?

At one level, the leaders of the UCS work-in were always anxious not to do anything too radical. They didn't go for a head-on fight with the Tory government. They framed their strategy to win friends and influence people, important people, rather than go for a short sharp showdown as the miners in 1972.

They wanted support and they got it. But they confined it within the fairly orthodox bureaucratic channels of the trade union movement. In the course of the UCS struggle the Communist Party did entertain one outside political focus. They revived an old favourite — the Scottish People's Assembly, a kind of mock parliament designed to bring religious leaders, SNP diehards, Tories and representatives of the millionaire Younger brewing family alongside celebrities from the Labour movement.

In the middle of a truly historic struggle, the Communist Party's politics led it to promote a contemptible operation. And this was done at a time when the most radical innovations were clearly possible. In the course of the UCS battle, organisations not unlike Methil's Council of Action were no mere pipe dream. If the UCS shop stewards had sponsored and initiated delegate right to work committees throughout the land, who can doubt that they would have met with a tremendous response? But the Communist Party was more interested in mock parliaments than the development and elaboration of real mechanisms for working-class power. And in the business of parliaments, mock or otherwise, the SNP is in an unrivalled position.

If UCS underlined the parliamentary pretensions and pre-occupations of the Communist Party today, the strike wave throughout central Scotland which followed Labour's return to office in 1974 showed the appalling price of seeking top positions in the trade union movement rather than building a rank and file movement.

The miners defeated the Heath government in 1974. Unfortunately the Tories' wage controls didn't go down with their captain. They were continued informally by the incoming Labour Government. Understandably, many trade unionists were unhappy with the way their wages were being held down. They began to express their concern in action. In Scotland, a series of 'unoffical' stoppages burst out at the end of the summer. By October and November, more than 40,000 workers had been involved in lengthy and bitter disputes for higher wages.

The strikes involved bus workers, lorry drivers, workers at the

Distillers Company, dustmen and engineering workers. Not all the disputes got support from the trade union officials involved. Indeed, the most obvious feature of the disputes was the way the national and local full-time officers fought to push their members back to work. In the main, the job of getting workers back inside the factories before they had forced any concessions out of the employers was carried out by the top, and reputedly left-wing, trade union officials such as Jack Jones and Hugh Scanlon.

In every fight their members were in, these two demanded an immediate return to work. The SMT workers were so sickened by their union leaders' response that they occupied the TGWU Scottish Region office in Glasgow and sent pickets to Transport House in London. These workers weren't 'extremists', just ordinary rank and file members being squeezed by their own union officers.

Throughout those Scottish strikes, the Communist Party paper, the *Morning Star*, contented itself with flat reportage offset by the occasional venture into enthusiastic description of some of the disputes. But there was never a word about the role of Jack Jones and Hugh Scanlon. The *Morning Star* never carried any advice to those involved in the disputes on how to link up and extend their action. It rarely carried detailed stories of the way the disputes were moving for fear of upsetting the trade union officials. On the only occasion it ventured comment on the direction and strategy of a particular strike, the advice given was to ignore the unofficial teachers' committees and to support the union machine.

Leading Communist Party members like John Reidford, secretary of Glasgow Trades Council, and Hugh Wyper, the Transport Union district official, constantly acted in the disputes to urge moderation or compromise, or plain surrender. In the dustmen's dispute, they urged the Glasgow men to go back to work and negotiate with the council. When the Labour Government moved troops in to break the strike and do the dustmen's job, the Trades Council could have mounted a campaign against the use of troops as strikebreakers that would have won over the trade union movement in the area. Instead, the Trades Council organised a demonstration that kept well away from the dumps and incinerators where the troops were working. While it was on, Hugh Wyper encouraged the strike committee to go back to the mass meeting and accept a return to work.

In the end, the movement to better wages and conditions that had grown in the Scottish strikes faded. The wage controls of the Social Contract had passed their first serious test. Faced with their Saltley, the Glasgow Trades Council leaders marched their troops in the opposite direction, away from the battle.

What could have become a credible campaign against any kind of wage control was never developed because the main organisation capable of giving it direction failed to do so. Many individual Communist Party militants played a tremendous part in building up the battle for wages.

But as a political organisation, the Communist Party failed because it was tied to the belief that the Social Contract wage controls would be headed off by left-wing officials rather than defeated by mass action. They therefore sacrificed a living movement for conference hall manoeuvres, an exchange all the more absurd since the success of the movement would have reached into every trade union conference hall in the land and more or less determined the outcome.

Today's struggles, like yesterday's, have one particular message for all those who really do want to change the system. It is not enough to have an approximation of the right ideas and policy. You must also have organisation, the ability to fight for your ideas in the heart of the movement and thereby gain at least an outside chance of winning through.

In UCS, more was possible than was achieved. In the first wave of the Scottish strikes in 1974/1975 the emergence of a real rank and file movement was within reach in Glasgow. At one time, five strike committees were holding separate meetings on the same issue in different rooms in the same building, the Trade Union Centre in Carlton Place. Had it been possible to unify those strikes, had Labour's army strike-breaking operation been stopped, who knows what possibilities would have opened up? Certainly the struggle would have broadened and deepened. The emergence of a credible socialist alternative would have come that much closer.

The years ahead will offer similar opportunities, and the possibility of seizing them. With energy and political flair, a new working-class party can be built. That organisation will match determination to change the system with a throughgoing internationalism which seeks allies among the exploited and oppressed of every country. Their solidarity alone can bring victory to the workers of Scotland, Wales or England, or indeed to the workers of any nominally independent country. That is why, in conclusion, we urge each and every one of you, our readers, who share our aspirations and concerns to join us in the Socialist Workers Party as soon as possible. Without your help it will not be possible to build the socialist alternative.

Harry McShane: No Mean Fighter
by Harry McShane and Joan Smith

Harry McShane's life is the story of the Red Clyde itself. He learned
his socialism in Glasgow's fiercely competing propagandist groups at
the beginning of the century. He served his political apprenticeship in
the anti-war struggles of 1914-18, and became a leader with a national
reputation in the unemployed workers' movement and hunger marches
of the twenties and thirties. Harry McShane survived the post-war years
of political apathy when the socialist movement was pronounced dead
if not buried, to participate at the age of eighty-odd in its resurgence
today.

Harry McShane told the story of his life and times to Joan Smith
over a period of three years. He remembers his school days in Glasgow,
his friend and comrade John Maclean, his entry into the Communist
Party and his break with it. He gives an uninhibited view of the giants
of the labour movement — Gallacher, McGovern, Wheatley, Maxton
and many others.

Harry McShane's story is, above all, the story of a warm-hearted,
cheeky revolutionary, who remained a revolutionary and who never
lost his roots in the Scottish working class.

ISBN 904383 24 5 paperback £3.00
ISBN 904383 29 6 hardback £6.60

Pluto Press
Unit 10, Spencer Court, 7 Chalcot Road, NW1